Presented To:

_____

From:

_____

Date:

_____

MONEY MYSTERIES FROM THE MASTER

GARY KEESEE

MONEY MYSTERIES FROM THE MASTER

Time-Honored Financial Truths From Jesus Himself

GARY KEESEE

DESTINY IMAGE® PUBLISHERS, INC.

P.O. Box 310, Shippensburg, PA 17257-0310

"Promoting Inspired Lives."

This book and all other Destiny Image, Revival Press, MercyPlace, Fresh Bread, Destiny Image Fiction, and Treasure House books are available at Christian bookstores and distributors worldwide.

For a U.S. bookstore nearest you, call **1-800-722-6774.**

For more information on foreign distributors, call **717-532-3040.**

Reach us on the Internet: **www.destinyimage.com.**

ISBN 13 TP: 978-0-7684-4011-9

ISBN 13 Ebook: 978-0-7684-9016-9

For Worldwide Distribution, Printed in the U.S.A.

5 6 7 8 9 10 11 / 19 18 17 16 15

ENDORSEMENTS

With all of the media madness and spin on the human understanding of finances, it is critical to have a book that unlocks the irrefutable principles of God for peace, protection, and provision regarding our God-given assets. This book propels Gary's passion in revealing to the world the inheritance we have in the financial plan of God.

Dr. Dean R. Radtke
Founder & CEO
The Ministry Institute

Sadly, the Church today is filled with get rich quick schemes, prosperity theology, and too many television evangelists looking for a handout. But Gary Keesee is the real thing. When he talks about money, I listen. He has the credibility, the experience, and the expertise that will change the way you think about money. *Money Mysteries of the Master* is the book you need to read—now. You won't regret it. Unless you have all the money you need for the rest of your life, then you need to get it today.

Phil Cooke,
Filmmaker, Media consultant,
Author, *Jolt! Get the Jump on a World That's Constantly Changing*

In his new book, *Money Mysteries of the Master*, Pastor Gary Keesee lays a solid foundation addressing the important issues of getting out of debt and moving into financial blessings. All the while he places top priority on staying faithful to the kingdom principles of faith and stewardship. Pastor Keesee provides Biblical and common-sense tools that break the bondages of debt and lack and enable people to walk in God's spiritual laws of blessing.

Marcus D. Lamb
Founder – President
Daystar Television Network

Together, Gary and I have discovered and lived these mysteries, experiencing their powerful impact in our finances and family, for the past thirty years. Gary shares these principles in a powerfully simple, yet life-transforming revelation, and I can attest he has lived them daily. We have measured our life and success by these timeless teachings from the Master Himself; I challenge you to do the same for real, measurable fulfillment and lasting achievement.

Drenda Keesee
Author, speaker and host of television Talk Show *Drenda*

CONTENTS

INTRODUCTION....................................11

Chapter One   A MYSTERY 19

Chapter Two   THE MYSTERY OF THE EARTH CURSE 33

Chapter Three   THE MYSTERY OF STRATEGY AND TIMING....47

Chapter Four   THE MYSTERY IS NOT A MYSTERY................71

Chapter Five   THE MYSTERY OF VISIONS AND DREAMS......81

Chapter Six   THE MYSTERY OF PRAYING IN THE SPIRIT.....97

Chapter Seven   THE MYSTERY OF PARTNERSHIP 107

Chapter Eight   THE MYSTERY OF PROFIT 127

Chapter Nine   THE MYSTERY OF THE ASSIGNMENT 137

Chapter Ten   THE MYSTERY OF A TRUST........................155

Chapter Eleven   THE MYSTERY OF THE MEASURE................167

Chapter Twelve   THE POWER OF FAITH..............................175

INTRODUCTION

MOST people enjoy a good mystery. I am sure I am not the only one who has watched a well-written mystery that presents evidence indicating one outcome, only to discover that I have been fooled over and over again because I don't have all the facts. Once all the evidence is revealed, a completely different conclusion becomes obvious. The twists and turns fool us because, again, we do not have all the evidence. The more twists and turns the writer of the mystery takes, the more we love it. We like the suspense of "whodunit" as long as it is just a story. But when it comes to living life, we can't afford to live with incomplete evidence. Our wrong conclusions can take us down a wrong turn for weeks, months, or years.

I know the frustration and pain of living in a mystery with no apparent solution, year after year. Although I worked hard, I just couldn't seem to make enough money to pay all my bills and get ahead. I was working in the financial industry, mainly selling life insurance and investments on commissions. I had mentors who were making hundreds of thousands a year doing the same, but no matter how hard I tried, I just barely made it through each month. As a month came up short, I would borrow against a VISA card to make ends meet, hoping that the next month I would find some great clients and be able to pay the money back.

My intentions were noble, but misled, as I found out. As I was unable to pay back the money on one VISA card, I was forced to open new accounts to borrow from. After a few years of living like this, I found myself in a financial pit, owing on ten maxed out VISA cards, three finance company loans, two car payments, back taxes, judgments and liens, and a $26,000 loan owed to relatives. Those were dark days. The pawnshop became a place for survival cash—we sold anything we had of value. Our cars were old, rusted, worn-out miracles. They were miracles because it was by the grace of God that they even ran—both had over 200,000 miles on them. Morning phone calls from bill collectors and attorneys came daily, since every bill we had stayed in the 120-day-late category.

We lived in a small farmhouse that was built in the middle 1800s, and it looked like it. Our family of seven barely fit in the house, with its dirt cellar, broken windows, one bathroom, and no closets. The sad thing was there was nothing on the horizon that indicated things were about to change soon. Bouncing checks was a way of life; going down to the IRS office to work out a payment arrangement was a way of life. Meeting the electric company's employee, who was sent to turn off the power every month, with a plea for mercy was also a way of life. But the greatest pain for me was being forced to say *no* to my wife and children: *no* to the braces they desperately needed, *no* to the lessons they desired, *no* to the new clothes that they would have loved, and *no* to about everything they wanted to do.

One of the most frustrating things to me at the time was that, as a Christian, I believed that God really wanted better for my family. We were faithful to our church, and we loved God. We were generous people and had a heart to give, not only to our local church, but to other people we saw in financial need as well. But for some reason, nothing ever changed—nothing, that is, until the day the van burned up.

Before I tell you that story, I want to be sure that you have a proper perspective of how long we had lived like this. The answer is almost nine years. I wish I could have said it was a little dip of a week or a month, but we had lived in financial crisis for almost nine years before the van burned up. So let me tell you what happened.

Like any given day at the Keesee home, we had our normal creditor calls asking if we had any money to pay toward the outstanding debt we owed them. Of course, all the credit cards had been canceled months before and now had been placed in collections. This one particular day was not out of the ordinary, except this time the call was not the average bill collector. It was an attorney who stated matter-of-factly that they were filing a lawsuit against us for the outstanding balance of one of the credit cards we had been trying to stall for several months. There was no mercy, no leeway, and no trying to talk this guy out of anything. After my usual plea for more time, he simply said, "Have the money to me in three days or the suit is filed," and he hung up.

The call hit me hard. Not that the call was that much out of the ordinary for our family at that time, but rather, it was a strong reminder that I was through. It was over. I had no credit left, no place to find money. I had exhausted all of my family and friends, and every card had been canceled. I had already sold most anything of value; there was nowhere to turn. I hung up the phone in despair. With tears in my eyes, I went upstairs to my bedroom, threw myself across my bed, and cried out to the Lord.

"God," I said, "what am I to do? Your Word clearly says in Philippians 4:19, *'And my God will meet all your needs according to His glorious riches in Christ Jesus.'* But God, my needs have not been met. What is wrong here? I know that You do not lie, so show me the reason why this Scripture is not true in my life."

Instantly, I heard His voice come up out of my spirit. "Gary, you trust in debt and the earth's system of finance. You have never allowed Me to teach you how My Kingdom works in the realm of money. When you need something, you do not pray with your wife about it or ask Me how to go about it; you simply use debt and trust that I will help you pay for it. Take the time to learn how My Kingdom operates, for most of My church is in the same situation that you are. They are living just as My people in the Old Testament were, as slaves under Pharaoh. My heart was to deliver them. My desire is the same today. I want My people free financially."

I got it! I saw it! It was my fault—not God's—that things were not working. I simply did not know how the Kingdom of God operated, but I could fix that. In my excitement, I ran downstairs and told Drenda what the Lord had told me. We held hands and prayed. I repented to her for my lack of leadership in the area of money, and we both committed to do whatever it took to learn how the Kingdom of God worked. Although nothing had changed in my situation, I felt 100 pounds lighter. Peace filled my heart. I knew that I had found my answer—the Kingdom of God.

Two days later, I headed to meet a client about his life insurance. In those days, I always parked my car around the corner from my client's house, never in front of the house. The minivan that I was driving had a slight problem. When started, it filled the driveway or street with white smoke, and I don't mean a little, either. I just always felt it would not help business if I parked in my client's driveway and upon leaving fill the driveway with smoke. I assumed my credibility in the area of finances might be slightly affected since I was asking clients to possibly invest hundreds of thousands of dollars with me.

This night was no different. As I made my way from my client's home that night, I was horrified to see that the man was actually following me down the street to my car. He meant nothing by it; we were just talking. But I was a little concerned that he would hang around while I started the car. We continued talking as I got into my van. With the window down, I continued to talk, hoping that he would say good-night and I could then act like I was doing something for a minute as he walked away, but he didn't.

Finally he did say good-night, but he simply backed away from the van and stood there. I knew I was had. I started the van, hoping maybe this one time it would not erupt in white smoke, but that was a wish that was not to be. Instantly, the air was filled with smoke that burned your eyes. The man motioned to me in a hurried way to turn off the van. He walked back over to the window and asked if I could put up the hood. He then went on to explain to me that he worked part time as an auto mechanic, and he wanted to check something out. After a minute, he came back and said, "Just as I suspected! You have a busted head gasket; drive the van home and get it fixed immediately."

I thanked him as I drove away, but his diagnosis meant nothing to me. I had no money to fix the van. My office was only about six miles from my client's home, and as I headed back toward my office, that familiar blanket of depression came over me. But as I was driving, I remembered what the Lord had said to me, and I began to talk to Him about my van. "Lord," I said, "I do not have any money to fix this van. I still owe money on it, and I cannot sell it broken. I just do not know what to do. Maybe it would be better if the van just burned up. That way the insurance company would pay it off, and I would be rid of it."

About three miles from my office, I saw a bubble forming on the hood. I'd never seen that before. As I watched, the bubble got bigger and bigger until, as I pulled into my office's parking lot, the bubble burst into a ball of flame. I thought, *God, did You hear me say that?!* I was in shock; the entire front of the van was now engulfed in flames that rose six feet off of the hood. I sat there stunned for a full minute until I realized, *Get out of the car, genius! This thing is on fire!* I quickly ran into the office building and called the fire department. Actually, the fire department was five houses down, but it took them 20 minutes to come, which was fine with me. Inside, I was cheering, *Burn, baby, burn!*

The next day, the insurance company totaled the van, and they gave me a check that paid it off, with enough left over to pay off the attorney who had called me three days earlier. Drenda and I were amazed. We did not know what to think. We knew that God was working for us and that something was changing. But our commitment to the Kingdom was about to be tested in a new way that would set our path for years to come.

After the van burned up, we were of course excited, until we suddenly realized, "We don't have a vehicle!" Although the van was now paid off and the credit card attorney was paid, we had no money to purchase a new van. Upon hearing of the loss of our van, my dad called and told us that he wanted to help us get a new van. We were excited as we heard that news. So my dad and I went to the local car dealership and found a van that Drenda and I liked. My dad generously offered to give us $5,000 toward its total purchase price of $17,000. However, that would leave us $12,000 to finance. I reluctantly filled out a credit application for the thousandth time in my adult life, and my dad cosigned for it. They said they would let me know in the morning.

That night we could not sleep. We knew that we could not take that loan. The Lord had just spoken to me about not doing such a thing again. But with no car the pressure was there for me to bend and give in. After a horrible night of sleep, Drenda and I agreed that we just could not sign that loan paper. I called my dad and thanked him for his gracious offer, but told him that we were going to decline. Next, I called the dealership and told them the same thing. They were disappointed, as the loan had been approved that morning, and the van was cleaned and ready to pick up. Although we had no clue as to how God was going to help us with our van, we felt a peace about it.

During that time period, Drenda had been selling a few antiques as she found them at garage sales and such. She had left a message for a man about buying several rooms of furniture that he had for sale. This was a month before the van burned up, but she had not been able to make contact with him. Finally, a couple of days after the van burned up, he called and agreed to sell these three rooms stuffed full of furniture to Drenda for less than $1,000. Drenda made an agreement with an auction company to sell the furniture for her. She was also able to negotiate the perfect commission—a good, used Peugeot station wagon that the auction company was going to sell.

Suddenly we had a good car that was paid for, the credit card was paid off, and the van loan was paid off. *Wow! So this is how the Kingdom operates!* At that point, we had proven to ourselves that God's system worked, and we committed to keep learning and using God's system from that point forward.

We went on from there and became completely debt free over the next two and a half years. Our lives drastically changed. We began paying cash for our cars. We also were able to leave the farmhouse and pay cash for our 55 acres of land where we built our dream home, which is also paid for. When we built our new home, the day they broke ground, Drenda and I literally cried and shook because we just could not believe what was happening. The basement alone was bigger in square footage than our little farmhouse. We continued to be amazed at what the Kingdom of God would do, and our vision grew for our future.

We started three companies, which 23 years later still produce millions of dollars in gross revenue every year. We were content running our businesses and sharing the Kingdom with people until 1995.

In 1995, God directed us to start a church in my hometown, a church that would teach people about faith, family, and financial restoration. We did not know anything about pastoring a church. But we knew what we had learned, so we simply taught the people about the

Kingdom and how it had changed our lives. We found out that a lot of people wanted to know what we had learned, and the church grew, requiring us to step out in faith again. We built the Now Center, an $8 million project. The Now Center serves as a community center for our area, and it's the home of Faith Life Church, where currently 1,500 people worship together each weekend.

Drenda and I just kept applying the principles that God taught us, and God kept leading us to continue teaching what we learned to more and more people. In 2005, God spoke to us to launch Faith Life Now, a television and outreach ministry. It was created to teach the principles of faith and the Kingdom to even more people around the world. The *Fixing the Money Thing* broadcast now reaches 550 million households worldwide every week, and we have had the honor of sharing the good news of the Kingdom with millions.

Faith Life Now currently hosts two weekly programs: *Fixing The Money Thing* is a program that equips people with knowledge on finances, the economy, success, and Kingdom principles; and *Drenda* is a women's talk show aimed at healing broken women, strengthening marriages and families, and bringing a voice of righteousness to today's perverted media culture, a culture that has been aligned against the family for a long time. We also launched Life Leadership College, a learning institution that focuses on marketplace ministry, business, and Christian counseling, as well as basic life skills.

As you can see, our vision is not slowing down. Once I started uncovering the mysteries of the Kingdom of God, I just could not stop telling people. And now God has led me to write this book in order to share with you the same answers that changed my life.

|||||||||||||||||||||||||||||||||||||||||||||||||||||||||||||||||||||||||||||||||||||||||||||||||||||||||||||||||||||||||||||||

Chapter One

A MYSTERY

PETER had a problem, a problem that is common with people in general. He needed some cash and fast. Peter had taxes to pay, and since he had left his fishing business to follow Jesus, he had to depend on Jesus and those who supported them for the money he needed to live. When he brought this problem up to Jesus, Jesus gave him a very strange answer. Jesus told him,

> ...Go to the lake and throw out your line. Take the first fish you catch; open its mouth and you will find a four-drachma coin. Take the coin and give it to them for my tax and yours (Matthew 17:27).

When I first read this story, I thought that Jesus was just demonstrating to Peter that he should trust Him. But now I know that there is much more there, insight into the Kingdom of God that, once learned, can meet any need. It will change your life, just like it did Peter's.

This is the mystery that we want to solve: why did Jesus tell Peter to go and catch a fish when he had taxes to pay? Why didn't He just tell him to go to the treasury or ask someone else for the money? Or why didn't He tell him where some money was just lying around on the street in the dust somewhere? Why a fish's mouth? There are two reasons why Jesus told Peter to catch the fish. One is the simple and obvious one—Peter knew how to fish. But the second reason was not so obvious. And *therein* lies the powerful mystery. Before we go further, let me tell you of a recent example that did not happen 2,000 years ago, but happened to a man I met.

Jerry sat across from me as we ate lunch. He had traveled to where I was doing a television interview to have lunch with me and to tell me what had happened to him after he had listened to a set of my CDs. Jerry had been in ministry for 30 years, but had to retire from active ministry because of a stroke that left him disabled. Unable to work, and finding his finances in shambles, he told me that one day he sat with a loaded .45 gun in one hand and a Bible in the other, despairing of life.

Down to his last few dollars, Jerry happened to see me on television and called in asking for my teaching that discusses the mysteries of the Kingdom of God. In that teaching he said he saw things that he had never seen before. Hope rose up as he realized that all was not lost. He then explained to me how he had released his faith for $2,000 that he needed desperately for some utility bills that were long overdue. He told me how he had taken $30 dollars, laid his hand on it as he prayed over it, and sowed it into the Kingdom of God, believing that God would show him how to get that $2,000. He wrote down on a piece of paper the time and date that he believed that he had received that much needed money by faith. He based that act on Mark 11:24 which says, *"Therefore I tell you, whatever you ask for in prayer, believe that you have received it and it will be yours."*

A week and a half later, a man Jerry knew, but had not seen for over a year, stopped by his house. After some small talk, the man said, "Jerry, the reason I stopped by today is because a week or so ago I was praying and felt a very strong urge to bring you this check for $2,000."

Jerry was shocked. The man went on to tell Jerry the time and day that he had such a strong unction to bring him the money and asked if anything was going on then. Jerry told me that he sat there in awe as he pulled the piece of paper out of his pocket where he had written the time and day that he had believed that he had received the $2,000. He handed the paper to his friend. The time and date on the piece of paper matched the time and day that his friend felt the urge in prayer to bring the $2,000 to Jerry!

Jerry went on to tell me how his whole life changed from that moment. He knew that what he had just witnessed was not a coincidence. They both now knew that what had just happened was the work of the Kingdom of God. But how? Why did it happen? What caused this to happen? Many people need money—Jerry had needed it many times in the past, but money had never shown up like this.

Jerry had seven children, and all but one were married or moved out. Only the 16-year-old was still living at home, and he wanted nothing to do with God because of the despair that he had seen in his father. Jerry knew that the son needed to see God's Kingdom function to bring the boy back to God.

In my Kingdom teachings, I tell how God taught me about the Kingdom and the laws that govern it through deer hunting. I know it sounds crazy, but I love to deer hunt, and we also needed the venison in those early days when money was tight. I would spend hours hunting with no results, until one day after our blue Dodge van burned up, which I wrote about in the Introduction, the Lord told me to trust Him for my deer. He told me what to do to receive my deer, and I went out and harvested that first deer in 45 minutes. This has happened now for 24 years straight. I tell people, "I don't hunt deer—I receive them." In fact, I even wrote a book called *Faith Hunt* to share how I learned about the Kingdom through hunting.

Well, Jerry told his son—who loved to deer hunt—about the principles of faith and how he could know, not hope, but *know* that he would get a deer when he went out hunting based on my teaching. Jerry also told his son about the financial miracle he had just witnessed himself. The son was intrigued. By committing the deer hunt to the Lord, the boy harvested a nice buck in eight minutes and was absolutely shocked. On the way to drop the deer at the meat processer, Jerry put one of my teachings in the car CD player. When they arrived at the meat processor's office, he asked his son if he wanted to go in, but the son said he wanted to listen to more of the CD. Jerry left the car running, and when he came back out to the car, his son looked at him and said, "Dad, I think we have missed a lot." Jerry began to weep as he told me that his son gave his heart back to the Lord after that experience.

Jerry then went on to explain to me how the $17,000 came in that was needed to get the house out of the upcoming sheriff's sale and how he had the opportunity to tell all his children about the Kingdom of God and the things he was learning. Jerry now conducts a weekly Bible study at his home and is teaching others about the laws of the Kingdom. Jerry also went on to explain how he had seen remarkable recovery from his stroke since he began to apply Kingdom laws, and he has lost 70 pounds and is getting stronger every day. He said to me, "I just had to come and thank you for teaching me about the Kingdom of God. Gary, I have pastored for 30 years and had never heard the things you taught me. It saved my life." I thanked Jerry for being so kind and reminded him that the laws of the Kingdom have been there all along for anyone to discover and use. They are God's principles, not mine.

Are the events of these two stories just a coincidence? Why did these things happen to these two men and not to others? Can these kinds of things happen for anyone today? My answer would be a resounding, "*Yes!*" These examples I have given you *both* happened as a result of spiritual laws. It wasn't because God just all of a sudden felt sorry for Jerry and decided to do something to help him. No, God's kingdom operates from laws of operation just like the earth realm does.

The laws that governed flight were always in the earth since creation, but no one was able to fly because no one had ever discerned, dissected, and utilized those laws up until the last century. Once those laws were understood and written down, they could be duplicated any time someone wanted to utilize those laws. In other words, anyone on planet earth can fly if they apply the laws that govern flight. But although those laws existed, they were a mystery for thousands of years. People could see that birds could fly, but no one really understood how they did it or the laws that made it possible for them.

In the same way, electricity has been in the earth since creation. But if I would have told a group of people in the year A.D. 200 that I was going to light their home with a little glass bulb, they would have thought that I was nuts. If they came into a modern home and saw how it was lighted from a little glass bulb, they would have said it was a miracle. But it was not a miracle; the light they saw was working just as it will always work for anyone who will take the time to learn and duplicate the laws that govern electricity. The same is true for all the laws of physics that govern the world we live in. They can be used by anyone at any time if he or she will take the time to understand and apply them. We can put our confidence in those laws—they do not change!

The Kingdom of God works the same way. There are spiritual laws that govern the Kingdom of God just as there are physical laws that govern the earth realm we live in, and they also do not change. You see, the visible is being held together by the invisible, and the visible realm can be no more stable than the invisible realm that holds it together. As Hebrews 1:3 says, *"The Son is the radiance of God's glory and the exact representation of his being, sustaining all things by his powerful word…."*

I was a Christian for many years and yet did not know the principles and laws of the Kingdom. As I travel and teach people about this

Kingdom, I am always amazed at the lack of knowledge that most people have regarding spiritual laws. Often people will approach me and say that their situation is just like mine used to be. What should they do? I will point them to Second Peter 1:3 and show them their answer.

> *His divine power has given us everything we need in life and godliness through our knowledge of Him who called us by His own glory and goodness.*

Peter tells us here that we already have access to everything we need to live life successfully. But how do we access it? Peter says it is through our *knowledge* of Him (the king) and consequently His Kingdom and how it functions. As we discussed, electricity has always been here for anyone to use since the earth began. We could ask, "Well then, who can enjoy the benefit of electricity in the earth realm?" The answer would be anyone who, first, has the knowledge that electricity does exist and, second, understands the laws that govern its use. Just as anyone can learn the laws that govern electricity, anyone can learn the laws that govern the Kingdom of God and utilize them at any time. For most people, the good news is that they are probably just a little bit of knowledge away from being able to put all the pieces together and have a breakthrough like my family did.

Many Christians do not have an understanding of spiritual law and think that they have to beg God and convince Him of what they need before He will respond. That is not true. God has already given us everything that we need for life when He gave us the Kingdom. The problem is that many, if not most, Christians do not realize the Kingdom of God functions and operates from spiritual law. Instead most people think that God just decides what and if something happens based on how He feels at the moment about their situation.

Because of this lack of knowledge, many people who belong to the Kingdom do without the benefits of living in the Kingdom. They are going to Heaven, of course, but they are missing out on a lot of the benefits in the here and now. And consequently, their testimony is weak to the unbelievers who live around them. Once we understand spiritual law, we can use the Kingdom any time that we need to. Just like turning on a light when we walk into a dark room, we can reach for the Kingdom when the need is there. Many times having knowledge of the Kingdom and its function is the difference between life and death. It was for Jennifer's baby.

Jennifer began attending my church and hearing about faith and the Kingdom. She was thrilled to learn of her authority and rights in the Kingdom as she was pregnant with her second child and she desired a home birth. So she began to study what the Word of God said about childbirth and the promises in the Kingdom that would apply to her child. She was convinced that she could have a healthy home birth. She lined up a midwife, and she asked one of the women of our church who had had a few home births if she would coach her. During the time preceding her delivery, she was at every service just soaking up the principles of the Kingdom. These concepts were new to Jennifer, and she loved learning that there were real answers in the Kingdom of God. Unfortunately, during this time, her husband had to work on Sundays and was unable to attend church with her very often. Well, it finally came time for the baby to be born. The midwife and the coach had been called.

It was about 2 or 3 A.M. when the phone beside my bed rang. On the other end, I heard Jennifer's birth coach screaming into the phone, "Pastor, please pray, the baby has been born dead!" The news jolted me awake. The birthing coach then stated that the baby had just left in an ambulance for the hospital. Drenda and I jumped up and dressed. I began to pray in the Spirit, listening for what I should do. I knew that the devil would love to slander my church with this event. I could see the headlines, "Baby Dies as Cult Church Encourages Home Births." We really did not take a stand on the issue of how a baby should be born, either at home or not, but many of the women in our congregation chose to have home births, and I knew that the enemy would love to make us look like a cult church. Drenda and I continued to pray in the Spirit as we were driving toward the hospital, which was a 20-minute drive. About halfway there, I suddenly felt the Spirit of God come over me, and I knew that the baby would be fine. At that exact second, my wife turned to me and said the Lord just told her that the baby would be fine.

I knew what the Lord had told my wife and me, so as I walked into the emergency room, I was curious as to what I would find. In the ER, I saw a group of about seven or eight nurses standing around what appeared to be a completely normal, pink, crying baby. I took a careful study of their faces. In most situations where a baby is being held by a group of women, you would see smiles. But this time, there were none. Instead, there was a look of shock on every face.

Meanwhile, a different ambulance had transported the baby's mother, Jennifer, to the maternity ward. Consequently, she did not know about the status of her baby girl. My wife, Drenda, went up to the maternity floor to check on her. As Drenda walked into the room where Jennifer was resting, she said, "Jennifer, your baby is fine, and she is just gorgeous." The nurse standing next to Jennifer jumped in and stated curtly, "No, that baby is in a body bag!" My wife very emphatically corrected the nurse about her error. Today, to the glory of God, the baby girl, who was named Haley, is a beautiful young lady with no brain damage or side health issues of any kind. I understood that God's kingdom operates out of spiritual law and that this result was not by chance. So being the spiritual scientist (not Christian Science, but someone who studies how the kingdom of God works) that I am, I wanted to find out exactly what happened.

I knew baby Haley had been officially declared "dead on arrival" by the ambulance crew that came to the house. I also knew that the baby was also declared dead on arrival by the hospital. So what happened? I talked to the birthing coach who was there and had called me about the emergency. I asked her to tell me everything in detail about what had happened. I was looking for clues. She said that everything with the birth had gone well until the baby was born. She had no vital signs and was deep blue in color. The midwife tried to revive the baby but could not. The coach went on to say that Jennifer had many of her family members there who then began to panic. But Jennifer calmly told them to be quiet, and she put her finger in her husband's face, stating, *"Don't you say a word—this baby will be fine!"*

I stopped the coach's story right there and asked her if she could repeat to me what Jennifer had said to her husband again. She told me the same thing she had just stated, that Jennifer had put her finger in her husband's face and said, *"Don't you say a word—this baby will be fine!"* Wow! That was it! That was the moment, the declaration that saved baby Haley's life. I felt like a detective who had just solved a major case! I was elated. It was so simple, yet so profound. Jennifer had simply applied a spiritual law in the midst of that situation, and it had saved her baby's life! After meditating on what I had just learned, it all made sense.

Jennifer knew that, due to his work schedule, her husband had not been built up in faith like she had over the preceding months. She also knew that, as the head of their home, his agreement with the horrifying scene at the birth would seal the baby's fate. That is why her first response was to speak to her husband and not allow him to come into agreement with the death of their child. Jennifer instead was convinced that the child would live and be fine, and she declared it with boldness and faith.

As soon as Jennifer was released from the hospital, she went to the ambulance crew and asked them what they had done for the baby after they came to her home that night. They looked at her with sheepish faces.

"Nothing," one of them finally offered.

"What do you mean, *nothing?*" Jennifer asked, "Did you do CPR?"

"No," they said.

"Did you do *anything* for the baby?"

"No," they said again.

They told her that the baby was simply dead, and they had no hope of her recovering. *However,* the baby just "woke up" when they arrived at the hospital! That ambulance crew received accolades from the hospital and firehouse for the response of the year, but they admitted they had done nothing.

We recently had Hailey on our television broadcast with her mother Jennifer, and all of us, with tears in our eyes, celebrated the Kingdom of God again. We celebrated the fact that someone was on the scene who knew how to operate within spiritual law.

I am trying to lay some groundwork in this chapter to help you understand that the Kingdom of God works just like the Bible says it does. The stories that you read about in the Bible still happen today. And since this book is about money, you may say, "Well, I do not know what the Kingdom has to do with money, and I certainly do not understand what Jennifer's story has to do with money." But Jennifer's story has a lot to do with money because her story is about spiritual law— and having money has a lot to do with spiritual law.

For many, the stories I am telling here are foreign to them. Most do not know that the Kingdom of God operates by laws that can be learned and used in life whenever *they* need to tap into the Kingdom for answers and direction. Most people feel like they have to beg and cry for God to do something about their situation. But the truth is that

God already gave us a means of escape 2,000 years ago when Jesus paid the price for us to have full access to the Kingdom of God. Begging for something you already have is useless. Jesus Himself said it was useless to beg God in Matthew 6:7-10:

> *And when you pray, do not keep on babbling like pagans, for they think they will be heard because of their many words. Do not be like them, for your Father knows what you need before you ask Him. This, then, is how you should pray: "Our Father in Heaven, hallowed be Your name, **Your Kingdom come, Your will be done on earth as it is in heaven.**"*

You see, God already knows what you need. His desire to help you is not the problem. But God is limited by His own Word when it comes to His ability to bring something to pass in the earth realm. Remember, God has to work through people who have the legal dominion over the earth realm. God gave this authority to humanity when we were created. Because of human authority in the earth, satan had to gain access into the earth realm through Adam, which he did by deception. Even though humanity has fallen, we still retain that legal dominion to rule the earth realm, either for good or evil.

So we see that when Jesus was teaching us how to pray, He stated that God already knows what we need—that is not the problem. Instead, Jesus instructed us how to pray, to pray Heaven into the earth. The will of Heaven can't come into the earth without a man or woman giving God the legality He needs to move in the earth realm. This is why faith is required in the hearts of people for God to bring His anointing and power into a situation. Faith is basically agreement between heaven and earth. As long as God can find a man or a woman in the earth who is fully persuaded that what heaven says is right (righteous) then God has legality and can move through that man or woman to affect change. We must always remember that God has given us the authority in any situation to bring about righteousness and overcome the enemy. God can't do it without us.

Understanding the Kingdom and how it flows in the earth realm is powerful and exciting. The benefits of the Kingdom are not limited to a few because Jesus told us anyone could use Kingdom law and affect change in their lives and in other lives around them.

> *In the morning, as they went along, they saw the fig tree withered from the roots. Peter remembered* [that Jesus had cursed it with words] *and said to Jesus, "Rabbi, look! The fig tree You cursed has withered!" "Have faith in God,"* Jesus answered. *"I tell you the truth, if anyone says to this mountain, 'Go, throw yourself into the sea,' and does not doubt in his heart but believes that what he says will happen, it will be done for him"* (Mark 11:20-23).

Peter was astonished at what had happened to the fig tree—a person killing a tree by simply speaking to it? When Peter asked Jesus how this happened, Jesus answered with an explanation of spiritual law, that if a man believes in his heart and speaks with his mouth, and believes what he says, power will be released into the earth realm. Jesus made it clear that this law would work for anyone who would use it when He said, *"if anyone…."* This is the law that Jennifer had tapped into when she spoke out that her baby would be fine. Her heart was convinced of what Heaven said about her baby in spite of what the circumstances said, and she spoke and released the Kingdom of God's power into that situation. It saved her child's life.

This same Kingdom that caused little Hailey to live and not die has the power to cause you to prosper with amazing results, as I have experienced in my own life. I have seen the Kingdom change the financial future of hundreds if not thousands over the years, in my own congregation as well as in the thousands I have ministered to at conferences and via television.

Before we continue, first I must be sure you know that it is God's desire to bless you financially. Jesus paid for it. And second, you must know that satan never wants you to prosper—*never!* I will show you why Jesus spoke in mysteries and parables and will unravel the mysteries of the money parables. When I am finished, I trust that your life will be completely changed as mine was. God is no respecter of persons; we all have access to the same Kingdom.

||||||||||||||||||||||||||||||||||||||||||||||||||||||||||||||||||||||||||||||||||||||||||||||||||||||||||||||||||||||||||||||||||||

Chapter Two

THE MYSTERY OF THE EARTH CURSE

TO have a proper understanding of money and the Kingdom in relation to the earth realm, we need to go back to the beginning, to Adam and Eve. I know you may think that this book is about to get boring, but hang with me here. What I am about to share is life changing.

We can all agree that when Adam was created he had no need to worry about anything. God created Adam at the end of the sixth day of creation, when everything was complete and ready for him on the earth. God's plan was that Adam would live in the seventh day with himself. Everything Adam needed was there, and he had an assignment—he was to rule over the earth. In fact, Hebrews 2:7-8 speaks of Adam:

> *You made him a little lower than the angels; you crowned him with glory and honor and put everything under his feet. In putting everything under him, God left nothing that is not subject to him....*

We can see here that Adam ruled the earth. It was his domain and his responsibility. However, satan wanted the authority in the earth realm and did not like having to live under the dominion of God's man, Adam. Knowing that Adam had the authority in the earth realm, he knew that he had to steal that dominion. So he deceived Eve into committing high treason against God's authority. And through Eve's deception, Adam chose to rebel. At that point, satan gained dominion over humanity and death reigned on the earth. Adam and Eve's rebellion resulted in kicking God out of the earth so that the earth became cursed. The effect this curse had upon Adam's life was recorded in the book of Genesis.

> Cursed is the ground because of you; **through painful toil** you will eat of it all the days of your life. It will produce thorns and thistles for you, and you will eat the plants of the field. By the **sweat of your brow** you will eat your food until you return to the ground… (Genesis 3:17-19).

Adam was left with the realization that he would have to make his own way in life, by his own painful toil and sweat. That curse is still here today; that cursed system is what we were raised in. I call it the "earth-cursed system of provision." Essentially, what the curse means is that if we do not sweat or labor in painful toil, we do not eat. Because of that curse, we all are trying to find money through our own painful toil and sweat. Jesus mentions this in Matthew 6:32 when He says that the unbeliever runs (with painful toil and sweat) after the things of life. That is because this is the only system the world knows in order to get its needs met. This mindset is deeply ingrained in all of us. It operates at the subconscious level and influences every decision we make in life. Let me give an illustration.

If I told you that you *had* to—not asked if you would *try* to—but said you *had* to have your house paid off in two years, what would you do? I know exactly what you would do. You would begin to formulate a plan to work longer, get part-time jobs, grit your teeth, and apply more sweat and painful toil to the problem, because *that is the only system you were trained in.* Because of this earth curse, everyone is tired of running after provision. We are all tired of sweating and laboring with painful toil for money.

We all want out.

That is what the lure of the lottery is all about. People are dreaming of finally having more than enough so they can stop running and being a slave to producing provision. That is why the show *Who Wants to Be a Millionaire* is so popular. It's why gambling appeals to people—it's money with no labor attached.

Because of this curse, Adam had to abandon his created purpose. He no longer could focus on his assignment of taking care of the earth, but instead, his waking hours were consumed with finding provision. He became a slave to that need. People who do not have money spend their time running after it, and those who have money hoard it away because the only way of escape from this cursed system of finances, the rat race, is to have more money than needed. Thus, those who have it are consumed with thoughts of how to keep it, and those who don't have it filter every decision through the mindset of finding it.

Fear entered the earth at this time and worry consumed the minds of people. Adam lost his vision for life. There was no vision except survival. He also lost sight of his assignment or what I would call his purpose. His purpose now was to run after money and just survive. In our day and age, people have what is called a midlife crisis when they look around and realize that half their life is gone and they have worked their entire life for a paycheck with no purpose. They do not know who they are or why they are here. Jesus gave us more insight into this earth curse system in the Book of Matthew.

> *No one can serve two masters. Either he will hate the one and love the other, or he will be devoted to the one and*

despise the other. You cannot serve both God and money (Matthew 6:24).

Essentially what Jesus was saying is that you will serve the master you trust to meet your needs. There is no middle ground. All of your decisions will be based on the system you trust in. Because of this, most people make their decisions filtered through finding and keeping money. Let me say this very clearly—until you fix the money thing, you will never find or discover your created purpose. As long as your decisions are wrapped around financial survival, you will never discover God's purpose for your life. And your money thing will never be fixed until you have more than enough money. I know that sounds impossible, but it is true. Until the financial pressure is gone, you cannot lift your head from the grindstone long enough to look at what is out there and why you are here on earth.

When Adam sinned and lost the Kingdom, so to speak, God gave him a picture of what would someday be restored. It was called the Sabbath, which was to be practiced every seventh day in remembrace of the seventh day of creation where the Bible says God rested. Remember, the seventh day was to be a day of rest, not because God was tired but because everything was finished on the sixth day, and creation was complete. God provided everything that people would need to live a life of peace and fulfillment on the earth.

Humanity lost that place of rest, but God had a plan of restoration He was enacting to bring people back to that place of rest, the place in which God had originally intended people to live, a place of provision and peace with Himself. The Sabbath day was a picture of that promise, and it gave people a picture of what life was supposed to look like. God commanded the children of Israel to keep the Sabbath as a reminder of what God had really intended for humanity and what He would one day restore. Besides it being the seventh day, there was also one very important detail God wanted to be sure people saw—they were not allowed to do any work on the Sabbath. That's right, *work*. They could not sweat or painfully toil on the Sabbath. So the Sabbath day was a day of rest, a day where toiling and working were not to take place, an oasis in a world of survival.

But how was the Sabbath day possible? They still needed provision on the seventh day, so how were they going to survive if they could not labor or sweat, the only way they knew how to live? The key would be the sixth day. The Bible says that the sixth day would produce a harvest enough to last for two days (see Exod. 16:29). This "having more than enough" concept was called the double portion, and it was really the only means of escape from the earth's cursed system of lack as it enabled rest on the seventh day.

Do you see it? The Sabbath was a picture of what God had first created for man where God himself had provided everything that man needed or ever would need, a place of more than enough. He had intended for people to live in that place of rest with Him forever. But Adam lost the rest of the seventh day because he lost the provision of the sixth day, the completed creation of God. But God had a plan to bring mankind back into that place of provision and rest, and it was illustrated by the Sabbath day. Colossians 2:16-17 tells us that the Sabbath day was a shadow of what God was going to someday restore back to people through Jesus Christ. When Jesus said on the cross, "*It is finished,*" He was stating the same words that God had spoken back in Genesis when the earth was completed and everything was in place for humanity. Jesus paid the price for us to be redeemed back into God's family with all the benefits of being sons and daughters of God. We now have access to a new Kingdom, a Kingdom full of provision which enables us to live above the earth-cursed system of lack and defeat, a kingdom of more than enough.

Hebrews 4:9-10 says, "*There remains, then, a Sabbath-rest for the people of God; for anyone who enters God's rest also rests from his own work, just as God did from His."* Here the writer of Hebrews is telling us that this Sabbath rest is available to us today and through this new kingdom there is a way to walk above the earth-cursed system of lack and poverty. This Sabbath rest then was not just for the Old Testament nation of Israel; it is for us also. In review, the Sabbath rest was only made possible by having more than enough, and that "more than enough" was made possible by the people receiving a double portion on the sixth day. In simple terms, the Sabbath day had provision so there was no need to sweat or toil for it. There was rest. Again, this Sabbath rest Hebrews talks about is available to us today through Jesus Christ. Look at what Isaiah had to say referring to this covenant that we now have in Christ.

> *Instead of their shame my people will receive a double portion, and instead of disgrace they will rejoice in their inheritance; and so they will inherit a double portion in their land, and everlasting joy will be theirs* (Isaiah 61:7).

Do you see it? We have been given the double portion—more than enough—through what Jesus paid for. Jesus himself stated in Luke 4:21 that He is the fulfillment of this Scripture in Isaiah 61. He set us free from the earth's curse and made us sons and daughters of God, now with access to the entire Kingdom of God—more than enough! Jesus spent three years with His disciples teaching them about this Kingdom and how it functioned. But they had a hard time grasping it since its laws were so completely different than the earth-cursed system they had grown up in. One story that I think illustrates this better than many is recorded in the book of Mark.

> *So they went away by themselves in a boat to a solitary place. But many who saw them leaving recognized them and ran on foot from all the towns and got there ahead of them. When Jesus landed and saw a large crowd, He had*

compassion on them, because they were like sheep without a shepherd. So He began teaching them many things.

By this time it was late in the day, so His disciples came to Him. "This is a remote place," they said, "and it's already very late. Send the people away so they can go to the surrounding country side and villages and buy themselves something to eat."

But He answered, "You give them something to eat." They said to Him, "That would take eight months of a man's wages! Are we to go and spend that much on bread and give it to them to eat?"

"How many loaves do you have?" He asked. "Go and see."

When they found out, they said, "Five—and two fish."

Then Jesus directed them to have all the people sit down in groups on the green grass. So they sat down in groups of hundreds and fifties. Taking the five loaves and the two fish and looking up to heaven, He gave thanks and broke the loaves. Then He gave them to His disciples to set before the people. He also divided the two fish among them all. They all ate and were satisfied, and the disciples picked up twelve basketfuls of broken pieces of bread and fish. The number of the men who had eaten was five thousand (Mark 6:32-44).

When the disciples came to Jesus and told Him of this problem, He said an amazing thing: *"You feed them."* The disciples answered from the perspective of any well-trained earth-cursed person, "That is impossible! Why, it would take eight months labor to pay for that much food." You see, the only option for the disciples was to view the problem through their earth-cursed system mindset of painful toil and sweat. In this case, they said it would take eight months of sweating to meet this need.

But Jesus used this occasion to demonstrate this new Kingdom to them. He first had them identify what they had. Not much, just five loaves and two fish. But Jesus said to bring those few items to Him. The Bible then says that He blessed it and gave it back to the disciples. A brief explanation of the meaning of the word *bless* will help us understand exactly what was taking place. According to dictionary.reference. com, the word *bless* means "to consecrate" or "to separate." To understand why Jesus had to bless the bread, we need to remember what we have previously discussed in regard to human authority and dominion in the earth realm.

Remember, man was put in charge of the earth, so anything on the earth as it pertained to mankind is under the legal dominion of humanity. So when Jesus blessed the bread, He was separating the loaves of bread from the government of mankind into or under the dominion of the government of God where God had the legal right to affect change. In simple terms, the bread and fish changed kingdoms. The result? The bread and fish multiplied, and all the people were satisfied. But they were more than just satisfied; they picked up more than enough—12 baskets of fragments.

These 12 baskets of fragments show us the "more than enough" principle of the Sabbath rest in operation. I am sure that Jesus gave these fragments back to the boy who had given up his supply earlier. This story has profound Kingdom insight. We can see that the Kingdom of God operates with completely different laws and operations than the earth's cursed system of lack and poverty that we have been trained in.

I am sure that the disciples were beside themselves with joy on that day. But they got to see the same event repeated again later as Jesus fed 4,000 people—with *seven* baskets left over this time. But the disciples still didn't get it. Were they perplexed? Yes. But did they get it? No. I do not judge them harshly, because I did not get it for nine years of financial slavery either.

> *The disciples had forgotten to bring bread, except for one loaf they had with them in the boat. "Be careful," Jesus warned them. "Watch out for the yeast of the Pharisees and that of Herod."*
>
> *They discussed this with one another and said, "It is because we have no bread."*
>
> *Aware of their discussion, Jesus asked them: "Why are you talking about having no bread? Do you still not see or understand? Are your hearts hardened? Do you have eyes but fail to see, and ears but fail to hear? And don't you remember? When I broke the five loaves for the five thousand, how many basketfuls of pieces did you pick up?"*
>
> *"Twelve," they replied.*
>
> *"And when I broke the seven loaves for the four thousand, how many basketfuls of pieces did you pick up?"*
>
> *They answered, "Seven."*
>
> *He said to them, "Do you still not understand?"* (Mark 8:14-21)

Of course they should have just answered, "No, we don't have a clue; we just do not get it, Jesus." We cannot blame them, because what Jesus was showing them was something that made no sense in light of their earthly training. They really were in a bit of shock at the Kingdom's impact, let alone did they have any idea how to operate in the Kingdom to produce those same kinds of results. Jesus clearly rebuked their worry and continued to train them concerning the Kingdom's operation as their answer.

I want you to stop and think for a minute about what we have just learned. If you were all upset because you had bills to pay, and Jesus showed up in your bedroom at night, what do you think He would say to you? Some of us may assume that He would come over and give us a hug and say something like, "I know this is tough. I never promised you life would be easy. Have you considered bankruptcy yet?" Of course not! I believe that He would gently remind you of His word and encourage you to remember how His Kingdom operates, to stand up and win the battle. I would even say a gentle rebuke might be in order. But I doubt He would tear up and say, "Group hug!"

So let's take this a bit further. It worked for fish and bread in the Bible, but will it work today? Absolutely. It worked for me, and it is still working every day. The only difference between now and when I first learned these things is *then* I had to believe God for a few thousand dollars, and *now* I have to believe God for millions of dollars every year to keep every aspect of my business and the ministry going.

Listen, the Kingdom works for anyone and everyone, and yes even for you. You can learn how it functions to change your life, too.

Tim met me at the front of the church one Sunday morning. I had never seen him before, but as he introduced himself he stated that he needed prayer. This occurred in 2008 at the peak of the financial crisis. Tim is an architect, and he had been let go from the firm that he had been working for due to the downturn in business. He simply asked me to pray with him about a new job, which I did. I found out that Tim was new to the church and although a Christian had never really heard much teaching concerning the Kingdom of God and how it worked before. He listened with keen attentiveness.

He found out we were going to be remodeling our children's auditorium, and he offered to draw all the designs needed for the build out, free of charge. He said he was sowing into his future and his new job. He had heard enough teaching at this point to know that he had to give God something to work with, just like those disciples did on that mountainside with the bread and fish. So for one whole month Tim drew and helped construct the build out in our Motion City children's wing. Throughout that process he kept looking for work, but there was no building going on in Columbus at the time, and no one was hiring.

It was during this time that the Lord began to encourage Tim to start his own company. It had always been his dream, but he had never considered it, especially now with everyone laying off architects and the construction industry basically shutting down. But the more he thought about it, the more he decided he wanted to try it. He had no client base to turn to, so he started making cold calls to builders.

Tim had a dream, that some day he would be able to design a home for the Columbus Parade of Homes. Every year the Columbus Parade of Homes looks for the finest builders in central Ohio to build their very best homes to put on display. Anyone who builds there is recognized as one of the top builders in the state. Of course every subcontractor and architect wants to contribute to the homes going in because thousands of potential clients will be touring them. Also, anyone who is anyone in the building trade is there, and there is no greater place to build business interests within central Ohio. Tim had sown into his future, and he was sure that he was to go ahead and start his own architectural firm, even though this was the worst time in history to start a firm considering the economic situation. But Tim was diligent with his phone calls, and one day he had a surprising conversation.

Tim cold-called a builder and was talking to him about his new business when the builder said he was looking for someone to draw the home he would be building in the Columbus Parade of Homes. Tim could scarcely believe what he was hearing! This first builder hired him to do the prestigious design job.

A few weeks later, Tim was having lunch with a builder who had brought another builder friend along. This builder stated that he also had landed a place in the Parade of Homes and that he *also* needed an architect. You can guess what happened next. Now Tim had *two* home designs in the Parade! That's really unusual for any architect, let alone a brand new firm. But that's not all...

A few weeks later, Tim received *another* phone call from a builder who said he too was building a home in the Parade of Homes and needed an architect. Incredibly, Tim was contracted to draw *three homes* for the Parade of Homes in 2010. The most amazing thing is that *there are only eight homes in the whole parade*. Tim was now drawing three out of the eight! This had *never* happened before in the history of the Parade, that one architect would secure that many home designs!

This is especially amazing during a time when the city was full of architects and architectural firms all looking for business. Tim even received an enviable award for exterior architectural design at the Parade. Since then, Tim's business has taken off. Tim has experienced firsthand the Kingdom of God producing in his life, and he shares what he has learned anytime he has the chance.

But not everyone is excited when we prosper. Satan hates it when we prosper and will try to keep us enslaved because he knows that money is influence. Worse than that, others may see how good the Lord is and turn to serve him. The devil has worked hard to corrupt God's character, telling people that God is unfair and a hard taskmaster. He knows that if people discovered the truth about God, he would not be able to contain the flood of people leaving his kingdom and going into the Kingdom of Light. Isaiah called the Kingdom *"good news to the poor."* I know firsthand that it is still good news today.

> *The scroll of the prophet Isaiah was handed to Him [Jesus]. Unrolling it, He found the place where it is written: "The Spirit of the Lord is on Me, because He has*

*anointed Me to preach **good news to the poor**..."* (Luke 4:17-18 emphasis added).

Although we all agree that the Kingdom is absolutely good news, especially the double portion that is available to us, there is a slight problem. First, no one is going to give you money in the earth realm just because you need it and second, Adam gave satan legal jurisdiction in the earth realm and satan despises you having money. Again, satan knows that money is great influence, and he really claims it as under his domain. A verse in Luke chapter 4 will help us see this more clearly.

> *The devil led Jesus up to a high place and showed Him in an instant all the kingdoms of the world. And he said to Him, "I will give You all their authority and splendor, for it has been given to me, and I can give it to anyone I want to. So if You worship me, it will all be Yours"* (Luke 4:5-7).

Here we see an important fact of the earth realm revealed—satan claims all the authority and splendor of the kingdoms of the world as his! He makes a claim to validate his offer to Jesus, saying these things are legally his since they were given to him. He is correct in stating that he has a claim on the authority and splendor of the kingdoms of the world, because Adam gave him that right. Satan makes a point in mentioning money here and attempts to lure Jesus with it. He mentions that he would give Jesus the splendor of the kingdoms of the world. The splendor of a kingdom is obviously its wealth. If we look at any piece of money, we will find an earthly kingdom stamped or printed on it. Money is a product of earthly kingdoms and the direct result of commerce in the marketplace. Basically, in the earth realm satan will do all he can do to keep us in poverty and bondage, running and sweating under the earth's curse just to survive. He does not want us to have the freedom to discover the purpose and destiny God intended for us, as that would be dangerous for him.

Since this book is all about money, we must understand and acknowledge that God has no money because money is a product of an earthly kingdom, as we have just stated. The United States of America prints money for the purposes of buying and selling. So if God has no money, and it currently can only be found in the earth realm under satan's dominion, how can we successfully obtain it? That is the mystery about to be revealed. Intrigued?

Chapter Three

THE MYSTERY OF
STRATEGY AND
TIMING

I spotted Dan in the back of the church, and he looked scared. I was not too concerned about him because he was obviously seated with my cousin, Jennifer. Throughout the service, I could see the pained look on Dan's face and knew that the only reason he was there was because Jennifer had asked him to come with her. My cousin Jennifer is a strong believer, a woman of faith. But I could tell that Dan, although a believer, was not accustomed to our style of worship with our contemporary choruses and raising our hands to the Lord. Months later, Dan talked to me about that service. He said that he sweat through his shirt that first Sunday and gripped the chair in front of him for dear life. But something caught his attention as I taught along the lines of faith and success. He needed both. And Dan kept coming back.

Dan was a farmer with 1,400 acres, and farming was not going so well. In fact, it was not even paying all the bills. So Dan was hungry for some answers. Over the next few months, he was faithful to attend church, and I could tell he was more relaxed. He even moved up a bit from the very back row. I ended up officiating for Dan and Jennifer's wedding, and they continued to grow in the Lord together. But things were still not going well on the farm, and Dan knew he needed to step out in faith on the teaching he was receiving. Jennifer tells of the morning when Dan came into the kitchen and declared they were going to double the amount they were giving to the church. Jennifer was surprised and excited to agree with her husband. Over the next few months, Dan and Jennifer were faithful to their new commitment to give at a higher level until things changed one day.

As a farmer, Dan said that he constantly got loads of advertisements in the mail. He would glance at the catalogs as he tossed them into the trash can. This particular day, Dan noticed a small 3 x 5 card with a sales pitch on it. He tossed it in the trashcan without thinking about it. But all of a sudden, Dan says he felt the Holy Spirit give him a thought about that card he had just thrown out. So he reached back into the trashcan and retrieved it. The card advertised a new piece of farming equipment that had been developed to increase yields using a new innovative concept in farming. The card stated a date and time for a seminar that would explain its use and benefits. Dan attended that seminar and ended up buying that little machine.

Using that machine (one of only a few in the state of Ohio), Dan's crops produced a great yield: 128 percent greater than the year before. Dan and Jennifer were thrilled! They were able to buy the two new cars they needed, get caught up on bills, and give thousands to our church, which was building a new facility at the time. Dan and Jennifer were convinced now more than ever of the Kingdom's power to affect change and were excited to see what the future held.

The next year, the unpredictable Ohio weather brought a drought to the area for most of the summer. As Dan's pastor, I watched his life throughout the growing season, knowing that the yield forecast was down because of the drought. We were doing taping for our television broadcast in October of that year, and I sent my television crew out to the farm to get some shots of the harvest. And what a harvest it was! In spite of the drought, Dan and Jennifer's crops did *even better* than the year before. In fact, it was their best yield ever.

The harvest was so good that Dan bought another farm and paid with cash. He told me that his dad, who had been a farmer all his life, would have needed 10 years to pay that farm off, but he and Jennifer had been able to pay cash for the new land. Dan also told me about an interesting conversation he had with the neighboring farmer, who had walked across the field to talk to Dan during the harvest. With despair in his voice, this farmer told Dan he was only getting 20 to 30 bushels of beans per acre. Concerned, Dan knew that his neighbor was not even yielding enough to break even. Dan then told this farmer that he was getting *80 bushels an acre*. This amazing difference in yields gave Dan the chance to talk to his neighbor about the things he was learning. This was the amazing story of two farms, side by side, divided only by a fence, but with two totally different results! It amazed Dan and Jennifer and again showed the Kingdom's potential.

The next year, Ohio's crazy weather was severely wet. Many of Dan's fields flooded out, and he had to replant some of them three times. Dan saw no way he could make a good profit with all the expenses required to plant three times. But in spite of the rain, Dan and Jennifer held on to the Word of God, trusting Him to help them prosper in their farming. But the yields were down at harvest time. This was the first time since Dan had operated using Kingdom law that they had actually moved backward in their finances.

That was until one day when Dan opened the mailbox to find a check for over $100,000, made out to them from their farm insurance company. They were shocked. They had not even *bought* crop insurance that year, so they called the agent. The agent said that he had assumed they wanted to renew the insurance, but had forgotten to call Dan.

Funny thing was, this agent had also checked *yes* on the box for flooded out crops, which Dan had *never* checked before in his life. To this day, Dan does not know why the agent would have checked it. But because the agent had renewed the insurance and marked the box pertaining to flooded out fields, their profits actually went up 4 percent for the year! Once again, at the end of the season Dan and Jennifer thanked God for the blessing of the Kingdom on their lives.

This past harvest marked the fourth year that Dan and Jennifer operated with Kingdom principles, and I asked them how things went. They again reported a record crop. Dan said they were able to expand their land holdings to 2,500 acres through another amazing story of favor, which Jennifer was eager to share with me. It seems that the farm next door to them was foreclosed on. It had been for sale before the bank took it in foreclosure, but the price, set at $40,000 an acre, was too high for Dan and Jennifer to consider. Once the farm was foreclosed on, Jennifer called the bank and inquired about buying it. The bank was intent on taking the farm to auction to gain a better price. Jennifer explained to the bank that they lived next door, had rented and farmed that land for many years, and would really love to buy it. She told them they did not need to take it to auction because they already had a buyer. But the bank would not consider their offer, stating firmly that it would be sold at auction and they were welcome to bid on it there.

Jennifer knew that if the land went to auction, it could go very high and they might miss it. But a few days before the auction, she felt a nudge in her spirit to talk to the bank one last time. She just felt in her spirit that the farm was theirs. So she emailed the banker, reiterating their desire to buy it. And guess what! This time the bank agreed to sell it to them, not for $40,000 an acre, but for under $10,000 an acre!

Now, only one problem remained. The purchase would require a down payment of $100,000, a sum which Dan and Jennifer did not have just sitting around at that moment. Dan and Jennifer were talking about this down payment when the phone rang. It was a man from the Farm Bureau. He told Dan that he had a check in his office for $100,000, a payment that Dan didn't remember anything about. Dan shouted for joy and quickly called the bank, "Yes, we are ready to close! I have the down payment!"

Dan and Jennifer's lives have changed drastically by walking in the Kingdom of God, and they are not about to stop.

In Dan's story, we can see how God works with us to produce the results we need in the earth realm. Since God does not have money in Heaven, He has to help us create or capture it here in the earth realm. God showed Dan the answer he needed through that little card that came in the mail. When Dan followed the leading of the Lord to buy that machine, he prospered. Dan said he was only the second farmer in the state of Ohio to own this new machine. What would have happened if Dan had the mentality that most Christians have when it comes to money—to just sit and wait on the Lord to bring it? Well, those Christians are going to wait for a long time because that is *not* how it happens.

Most Christians operate in what I call the "mailbox mentality," thinking that someone is going to come by and say, "Hey! The Lord told me to give you this million dollars." Well, although those types of things have happened, they are extremely rare. Instead, we need to have a mindset of looking for opportunity. Remember, we have to harvest or capture wealth in the earth realm. God works with us to bring us to an intersection of opportunity (clue: look for a problem to solve) and then gives us a plan to capture it.

In First Samuel 17, Israel found herself outnumbered by a superior army that was threatening to take the entire nation as slaves. The Philistines felt sure they were about to bring an apparent slaughter to the Israelites, so they offered to allow one man from each army to fight to the death. This one match would determine the fate of either army. The problem was that the man the Philistine army chose to represent them was Goliath, a nine-foot-tall giant who had been trained as a warrior all the days of his life. There was no one in the nation of Israel who could stand up to Goliath and expect to win—at least by physical strength alone. The entire army, including King Saul, was quaking in fear.

But not David, a young shepherd who just happened to visit the front lines. He was there to bring rations to his brothers and to hear Goliath ranting about how no one would be able to defeat him. Instead of being afraid like the rest of the army, David couldn't believe his good fortune. He saw it as an *opportunity to prosper*. He asked all who were there what the king would do for the man who defeated Goliath. They all said the same thing: the person who took care of Goliath would get the king's daughter in marriage, his family would be exempt from taxes, and he would get great wealth (see 1 Sam. 17:25-27).

David's confidence was in the Lord, but he also understood that he would have to go out with God's help and capture that opportunity. That is why I say many times it takes more courage than faith. Faith brings us to the opportunity and courage takes us on over. We all know that David won the match and cut off Goliath's head, but how he won that match is the mystery that we must understand if we are going to prosper in the earth realm. This story illustrates one of the greatest money mysteries in the Bible, so let's take a closer look at it. Again, David was only a youth when he faced Goliath. His experience with fighting had only been as a shepherd warding off wild animals that were trying to steal his sheep. Goliath, on the other hand, had been a warrior from his youth and was skilled in using a sword, shield, and proper battle equipment.

David had no idea how to approach this battle at first. He tried on King Saul's armor, but David did not feel comfortable with it on. "I cannot go in these," he said to Saul, "because I am not used to them." So he took them off. Then he took his staff in his hand, chose five smooth stones from the stream, put them in the pouch of his shepherd's bag, and with his sling in his hand, approached the Philistine. Goliath was baffled by the scene before him. A boy was walking toward him with *no armor and just a staff.*

Goliath yelled out, *"Am I a dog, that you come at me with sticks?"* (1 Sam. 17:43).

> *As the Philistine moved closer to attack him, David ran quickly toward the battle line to meet him. Reaching into his bag and taking out a stone, he slung it and struck the Philistine on the forehead. The stone sank into his forehead and he fell facedown on the ground* (1 Samuel 17:48-49).

David won the battle! That's where most Christians call it a nice Bible story and move on. But as a spiritual scientist, I wanted to know what really happened here? Very simply, Goliath was taken off guard by a unique strategy and a boy who trusted in God. When David approached Goliath, Goliath could not figure out what was going on, because it made no sense to him. If David had tried to defeat Goliath with proper battle gear, he would not have stood a chance. His true weapon was a unique strategy the Holy Spirit gave him. But the strategy would have been useless if David had not done one more thing. The Bible says that David *ran quickly* toward Goliath. What would have happened if David had danced around for about 20 minutes getting his nerve up to engage Goliath? Goliath would have eventually figured out that David had a sling as his weapon and would have compensated with his shield accordingly. David won by using a unique strategy and also implementing that strategy in a timely manner.

Write these two words down somewhere: *strategy* and *timing.* These are essential in the spiritual battles that God will lead us to. But why are strategy and timing so important? What we are about to uncover is, in my opinion, one of the greatest mysteries in the Word of God. It's a mystery we must know if we expect to capture the valuable money opportunities God will show us.

> We do, however, speak a message of wisdom among the mature, but not the wisdom of this age or of the rulers of this age, who are coming to nothing. No, we speak of God's secret wisdom, a wisdom that has been hidden and that God destined for our glory before time began. **None of the rulers of this age understood it, for if they had, they would not have crucified the Lord of glory** (1 Corinthians 2:6-8).

Notice that the Bible says that if satan had figured out the plan of God, he would have never killed Jesus. Do you see it? The devil would have adjusted his strategy if he had picked up on the plan of God. This is as true for you as it was for Jesus and for David. Satan will also adjust his strategies against you if he can pick up on God's plans. Remember what I am about to tell you. God's primary tactic against the enemy is to surprise him with unusual strategies, which God gives a man or woman in the earth to bring His will in any given situation.

We can clearly see in David's case that the victory was accomplished by using an unusual strategy, a plan that caught the enemy off guard. Many Christians do not understand this vital law of spiritual warfare. If they do have some understanding of it, they procrastinate moving on it, losing valuable time and tipping off the enemy. By the time they move on it, they find all kinds of issues and problems because the enemy has had time to line up interference against it. As in David's case, it was not only the unusual strategy that caught Goliath off guard, it was that fact that David did not give Goliath time to figure it out. He *ran* to meet Goliath. So let me say it again, *one of our key weapons against the enemy in any arena is first using a unique strategy that the Holy Spirit gives us. Second, we must act quickly once the plan is revealed to us so we do not give satan the chance to figure it out.*

For instance, I was in severe debt. I was the poster child of what *not* to do with money. However, when Drenda and I made a commitment to the Kingdom and began to gain knowledge of how it worked, we had no more money than when we knew nothing about how the Kingdom operated. Why? Because, as I said before, God does not have any money; money has to be created or captured in the earth realm. But God does know where the money is and can give us a plan to capture it just like He did for David. In my case, God gave me a dream one night to start a company that would help people get out of debt. God gave me this plan while I still had lots of debt to pay off. That made a lot of sense, didn't it—me helping people get out of debt? Well, God was using the foolish to confound the wise. When God uses the foolish, it also confounds the enemy, who is not anticipating that strategy. The devil never had a clue that I would someday be out of debt *and* declaring the good news of the Kingdom in the area of money. *Neither did I,* but as we followed God and let God show us how to proceed, it worked!

People ask me all the time what they should do to win in life. I usually first ask a bunch of questions to discern the facts. But I tell them it always comes down to a plan, a unique path to run on, a niche that God will give them to own and occupy as theirs. At first that plan doesn't make sense. Usually the person has never before thought of doing what God shows them to do. Exactly! The devil has never thought of it either, so slip under his radar and go capture new territory. The next question people ask is how to hear that strategy? Well, that really is not that hard once you understand that the Holy Spirit is in you and that there is nothing that He does not know. Before you finish this book, I will make sure you know exactly how to do that. But before I do, there are a few more things that you must understand.

I want to go back to the question I raised in the Introduction: why did God tell Peter to go and catch a fish to pay his taxes? Why didn't He just pay the tax from the ministry treasury? I believe that He was teaching Peter some very valuable insights into how the Kingdom works so that Peter could continue successfully after Jesus left him. As I said in the Introduction, there are really two reasons why Jesus used fishing to teach Peter about the Kingdom. One of the reasons was obvious— Peter knew how to do that; he was a fisherman.

But the second reason is where the mystery and the victory are found. Who would have thought of catching a fish with a gold coin in its mouth? Peter had caught a lot of fish and sold them for gold before, but he had never caught a fish with gold in its mouth. So again, why did Jesus give that direction? This is the question that needs to be answered. I can give you the brief reason by asking you a question. If Jesus would have told Peter to go to the street and pick up a gold coin at so and so street corner, what could have happened to the coin? You're right; someone else could have picked it up. So here is the mystery: the coin was hidden *from the enemy* in a fish's mouth *for* Peter to catch. We can be sure that satan would never have figured that one out on his own. So write this mystery down.

Your answer is hidden from you, for you!

What I mean by that is that God works undercover in the earth realm. If He did not, we have already seen that satan would be tipped off and move to intercept the plan of God and spoil it. So our strength is the Holy Spirit giving us unique strategies to capture hidden treasures, plans, and opportunities. Paul tells us how this works in the following passage.

> *We do, however, speak a message of wisdom among the mature, but not the wisdom of this age or of the rulers of this age, who are coming to nothing. No, we speak of God's secret wisdom, a wisdom that has been hidden and that God destined for our glory before time began. None of the rulers of this age understood it, for if they had, they would*

not have crucified the Lord of glory. However, as it is written: "No eye has seen, no ear has heard, no mind has conceived what God has prepared for those who love Him" but God has revealed it to us by His Spirit. The Spirit searches all things, even the deep things of God. For who among men knows the thoughts of a man except the man's spirit within him? In the same way no one knows the thoughts of God except the Spirit of God. We have not received the spirit of the world but the Spirit who is from God, that we may understand what God has freely given us. This is what we speak, not in words taught us by human wisdom but in words taught by the Spirit, expressing spiritual truths in spiritual words. The man without the Spirit does not accept the things that come from the Spirit of God, for they are foolishness to him, and he cannot understand them, because they are spiritually discerned. The spiritual man makes judgments about all things, but he himself is not subject to any man's judgment: For who has know the mind of the Lord that he may instruct Him? But we have the mind of Christ (1 Corinthians 2:6-16).

I could write an entire book on this passage alone, but for now I want to point out a mystery to you. Let's look at one section of this Scripture:

*No, we speak of God's **secret** wisdom, a wisdom that **has been hidden** and that God destined for our glory before time began. **None of the rulers of this age understood it, for if they had, they would not have crucified the Lord of glory.***

The Word of God tells us that God's wisdom had to be hidden; it was secret wisdom. My question is, who was it hidden from, and why was it hidden? It is obvious in the context of the Scripture that God's wisdom was hidden from satan. It is also evident that this wisdom was not meant to stay hidden, for it was hidden for our glory, meaning that it was hidden from satan, but is for us to know. Again, as we have already discussed, if satan had understood the plan of God, he would not have killed Jesus. Or in other words, satan will adjust his strategies once he picks up on the plan of God.

This principle does not just apply to Jesus, but to any believer who is operating in the earth realm and desires victory. In regard to Peter's fish and the coin, Jesus was teaching Peter that he would have to trust the leading of the Holy Spirit to direct him with divine strategies in order for him to succeed in his ministry later on. So we could say it this way: the gold coin was hidden from Peter, for Peter. God knew where the coin was, but satan did not. If the coin had been out on the street somewhere, it would have been open to detection and would have been lost to someone else picking it up.

Besides the location and method that Jesus told Peter, He also gave a very specific instruction about which fish would have the coin in it. Jesus told Peter that he was to take the *first* fish he caught. Here is another part of the mystery that you need to understand. We mentioned it earlier in reference to David, but it applies here, as well. Remember, the Bible said that David ran to meet Goliath. I pointed out that this did not allow Goliath time to figure out what was going on. If David had taken a lot of time running around Goliath instead of running to engage him, Goliath would have figured out David's strategy. But because he *ran* toward Goliath, Goliath never had time to observe and change his plans.

Once we receive revelation and start to move on it, satan picks up on our actions. Although he can only react and does not know the plan of God, he does pick up on the direction and the anointing. So once Peter acted on the direction Jesus gave, it became apparent to satan. But just because it becomes apparent does not always mean that satan is aware of anything going on out of the ordinary. Peter fished all the time. It just meant that what Peter was doing was open and now being watched by the enemy.

Again, why the first fish? Although fishing was a normal thing for Peter and would not be unusual for him to do, once he began to dig in the mouth of every fish he caught looking for the gold coin, satan would have figured out that something was going on with those fish. Knowing that Peter was one of Jesus' disciples, it meant he would be watching all the more closely. At first satan would not take too much notice if Peter dug around in the mouth of a fish he caught. But if this continued, he would want a closer look. The moment that satan suspected a divine plan in operation, he would have tried to bring interference to Peter's fishing adventure.

God's plan for you is to always keep the enemy a day late and a dollar short through giving you unique strategies. By the time the enemy figures it out, it is too late. This is why Jesus said the coin would be in the *first* fish that he caught. Satan had no time to realize what was going on. Because God is always moving undercover until the moment of victory, you need to remember that **God's plans are always specific in location, method, timing, and operational detail.**

Many spiritual battles are lost in this arena. We have all tipped our hands before and have seen interference spring up from the most bizarre people and places. The mistake that most people make is that, when they hear an idea, a direction, or a plan from God, they immediately go out excitedly and begin to tell everyone they know what the Lord has told them. Sounds like Joseph boasting to his brothers, right? Of course if we start blabbing about the plan, the enemy picks up on it, and pressure and trouble come to steal the Word, as recorded in the Parable of the Sower (see Matt. 13). Thus, the plan either fails or is much harder to carry out than it should have been.

In the first chapter of Luke, when the angel appeared to a priest named Zechariah and told him that his wife Elizabeth was going to have a son in her old age, Zechariah responded, "How can I be sure of this? I am an old man and my wife is well along in years?" The angel Gabriel then said, *"And now you will be silent and not able to speak until the day this happens, because you did not believe my words, which will come true at the proper time"* (Luke 1:20). What happened here? Because Zechariah could have messed up the plan of God with his mouth, the angel made sure he was unable to speak until the child was born.

I have heard many times that God shows up at the midnight hour. I myself would be frustrated at times when it seemed that God was nowhere to be found in the midst of my pressure. But this fact works in our favor. God shows up at the midnight hour so that the enemy will not pick up on the plan of God to fulfill the plan or direction that He has given one of His servants until it is actually needed. Let me give you an example.

The day had started off with a lot of stress. I had a guest minister coming in town later in the day, and I was running so far behind on everything. Then my secretary called me with the bad news, "Pastor," she said, "we are $13,000 overdrawn today, and we can't make payroll. What should I do?" The words jolted me out of my dazed and tired mindset. I had been giving out, traveling, sharing the Gospel of the Kingdom whenever I could, and I was growing weary. Reluctantly, I said that I would put $13,000 of my own money into the church account to cover payroll. She then went on to explain that the television department did not bring enough money in that week, and that's what had caused the shortage. I thanked her for calling. I could tell she was also a little frazzled by the battles we were all fighting as we launched our new television broadcast.

I knew there could be times like this when I said "yes" to God regarding the television expenses. But that week I had already dealt with some cash flow issues at one of my businesses, and now when this call came, it was just more stress than I wanted that week. Oh, I had the $13,000—that was not the problem. But for some reason, that day I just started to feel sorry for myself. I did not want to talk to anyone. I did not even want to greet my minister friend at the airport.

Finally, after a long day of frustration, I did sit down to dinner with my friend who had come in to preach, but I just could not fake like I was having a great time. I told him of my day, knowing that he had days like this, as well. He began to encourage me and to tell me what I already really knew, that God was faithful and would provide the needed money. At that moment, my cell phone rang. It was one of my elders, and he said something like this. "Pastor, I am sorry I did not call you this morning, as I know I should have, to tell you a member of the church handed me a check for $20,000 early this morning for the television broadcast. I was just going to give it to you Sunday, but the Lord clearly told me that I was to call you and let you know about the check." I sat there for a moment a little stunned, and then I felt so foolish. God had indeed provided the money. We were not overdrawn as it had appeared. God had sent the money right on time.

My builder called one day toward the end of construction on our new facility, the Now Center, and said he had a bill that needed to be paid urgently. He said that he had known about the bill, but had failed to tell us about it, and now they wanted to be paid by the upcoming Friday. I asked him how much I needed, to which he replied, $90,000. Wow, some of you know how it is to build a house. It sucks every penny you can find out of savings, and that was our condition at that time. We just did not have that money in the bank. The call came from my builder on Tuesday morning, which gave us until Friday to find that kind of money. But amazingly, a check came in the mail on that Wednesday from a guy who had not been in church for a while, and of course he knew nothing of this bill. The check he sent was for $100,000.

This has happened so many times that I cannot count them. The point is that these were not "close calls" like they appear. Those checks showed up on time. God is not nervous or fearful in these types of situations, as we may tend to get. Instead, God is working behind the scenes with perfect timing to insure that the enemy does not pick up on the plan and bring interference to stop it.

In the same way, God only leads us with partial dreams and visions of our future, just enough to keep us moving in the right direction until we are mature enough to occupy the plan of God. He never shows us the whole plan; this is for our good. Once we get comfortable with how God operates in the earth realm, we can relax in tough times, knowing that God is aware of everything going on and will lead us at the right time and season into victory.

Again, another major money mystery that we must understand if we want to insure victory is the mystery of *timing*. When I refer to timing, I am referring to knowing when to tip our hand to the enemy and act on our plan. As we have seen in the preceding stories, timing is part of the strategy. Matthew 13:44 reads,

> *The kingdom of heaven is like treasure hidden in a field.*
> *When a man found it, he hid it again, and then in his joy*
> *went and sold all he had and bought that field.*

This Scripture reveals a different aspect of timing than what we have already covered. We find here what we could call the mystery of *preparation*. This Scripture compares the Kingdom of God to treasure! It is referring to the treasure of being able to hear answers, direction, and wisdom out of our spirits. For instance, "Should I buy that stock or wait?" "Should I sell my home or not?" Business ideas and concepts all flow out of this Kingdom on the inside of us. We have already talked about picking up on these mysteries in a previous chapter, and I'll cover it in greater detail in Chapter 6, but this verse gives us greater insight concerning knowing when to act and reveal our hand to the enemy.

Again, we note that the Word of God says these treasures are hidden. From our previous discussion, we know that these treasures are hidden from the enemy. We can also confidently assume that the analogy of the field in this Scripture is the heart of a person, or their spirit. We can assume this because in Mark 4:3 Jesus teaches a parable about the Kingdom of God using this same analogy, and Jesus Himself tells us the meaning of the field or ground as representing the spirit of a person. Since Jesus is again teaching about the Kingdom of God, we can assume that this Scripture carries that same explanation.

When this Scripture says that a man finds a treasure, it refers to the moment we receive revelation of something we need from out of our spirit, the ground. When we think of treasure, we usually think of gold and silver, but in reality, treasure is really what we need at the moment—an answer, a direction, an idea, and so forth. Now notice an important point. The man does not go out and start telling everyone about what he has seen; instead, the Bible says he hides the treasure again. So we see two things—first, the treasure is already hidden and then is found. Once found, it is again hidden, but this time by the man himself. When we ask why the man hid it again, the Bible answers that question. It says that he went and sold all that he had and then purchased that field. In other words, he was not in the position or did not have the means at the moment he found the treasure to actually take possession of it. So he enacted a plan prompted by the desire he had for the treasure to put him in a position to occupy that land and have the treasure at a later date.

There is so much wisdom in this Scripture. Many people, not understanding this mystery, make major mistakes that have caused great loss by missing the timing for the strategies that God gives them. When God shows us a glimpse of our future or even shows us part of the plan, we need to be mature enough to know that what we have seen has been revealed to us in order to set us on a path of intersection with our destiny and the treasure's occupation. Remember, destiny is not something we do, but a place we are called to occupy. *The key to destiny is preparation*, something esteemed as invaluable for those who find themselves in the day of battle or decision.

This Scripture teaches us that God will show us glimpses of a treasure that could be concerning our revealed purpose and destiny or an opportunity that is before us to capture. However, we must discern the timing. Are we able to occupy the treasure that was revealed? If not, we must prepare for a later date when we will be able to do so. If we foolishly try to occupy the treasure too soon, the enemy will bring pressure against us where our immaturity will not be able to stand. If we also foolishly begin to boast of the treasures we have seen too soon, the enemy is again tipped off and will make our journey much more difficult, if not impossible, to successfully finish.

So remember, there is the process of occupation, and it's a path that God will lead you to walk. Satan will tempt you to prematurely move toward your destiny. Be wise—do not mistake the beginning for the end! Walking in divine timing is just as important as having the plan itself. Trust me, you do not want the end at the beginning.

Early in my ministry, when our church was small, numbering around 200 people, I was praying one day and had a vision of me doing television. Now that was the farthest thing from my mind. The whole concept of me being on television was totally out of character for me. Although I saw the vision, I had no clue what it meant, but a seed was planted. Years later, as we were preparing to build the Now Center, we would send teams out across the state to look at buildings to get ideas to use in our new building.

On one particular day, I drove to Mansfield with some of my team to look at another ministry's building there. They were very helpful and took us on a tour of their facility. Everything was going along just fine until the person leading the tour casually stated, "Oh, here is our media room where we produce our weekly television show." When she opened the door to the studio, although we did not go in, the anointing came on me in a huge way. I began to shake, and the Lord said to me, "You will have that also." I was so shaken that I left the tour and went out and sat in my car. Again, these are glimpses or treasures that the Lord shows us. It was not for that season, but the Lord was preparing my heart to say *yes* when the season showed up.

A while later my wife attended a women's conference where a stranger sat down next to her and stated, "Are you guys doing television?" My wife stated, "No, but the Lord has showed us that someday we will." This lady then said, "When you get ready to do television, make sure you call this guy." She then handed my wife the name and contact information for the man who did their television work. My wife tucked the note in her purse. You have to know that we knew nothing—I mean *nothing*—about television!

A month or so later, as my wife was sitting at her desk, she came across that little note and thought, *I have nothing to lose. I think I will email this guy.* So she did, and he responded, asking her to send him some of my material. The next thing I knew, he was on the phone and wanted to talk to us about doing a television show. We met him briefly in Dallas, and he gathered some more information from us and said he would let us know what he proposed. To make a long story short, he flew out to our home in Ohio, which is out in the country on a dirt road, and he talked to us about television. We had never heard of him because we knew nothing about television, but when we talked, we found out that he has worked with every major ministry in the U.S. I thought to myself, *How did you get to my house? How is this happening?*

He proposed a broadcast plan, and I about fell out of my chair at the cost. I never realized that television was so expensive. I saw *no way* we could do television. We were in the midst of building the Now Center, an $8 million dollar project, and Drenda and I had just emptied our bank accounts and committed to give the project $200,000 ourselves. Now I was presented with a $250,000 contract for television that Drenda and I would have to sign and pay for personally. On top of that, we would have to have a $30,000 software database, plus new equipment, sets, and so forth. Drenda and I would have to come up with $300,000 to $350,000 out of our pocket in the next 12 months!

In my spirit I felt the Lord saying to go for it, but in my flesh I was shaken. I just did not see a way to pay for that out of our personal cash flow. My businesses were not projected to do enough in net profit to cover payroll, continue to expand, *and* have an additional $350,000 in net profit that year. I knew God could do anything, but I just couldn't see it. But God has His way of speaking to us in times like this.

A few months before I faced this decision, I had done a conference in Columbus, Ohio, and someone had given me a gold coin in the offering. I had never seen a gold coin before. When I picked it up, the Lord spoke to me and said, "As I showed Peter where the money was for his taxes, I will show you where the money is." At the time, I had not known what that word was meant for, but I sure did now! Drenda and I had just given $200,000 to the Now Center, and now only a couple months later, God was asking us to sign a contract obligating us to $350,000 for television costs over the next 12 months.

The Lord knows what is going on and what He has put in motion; we simply need to hear His voice and obey. Sometimes, however, our flesh just wants to throw a temper tantrum. And sometimes we have to handle our flesh like a 2-year-old throwing that tantrum—we have to confront our flesh and make it get in line. In this case, Drenda and I were scheduled to be in Maui for a couple weeks on a business trip. When I came home, I would have to have the answer concerning that television contract. I carried that gold coin with me to Hawaii to remind me of what the Lord had spoken to me as I prayed about that contract. However, even though I had the gold coin to remind me of what God had spoken to me, and even though I saw God putting together the television personnel and all the contacts to start this new venture, I was *miserable*. In fact, I started feeling sorry for myself.

"After all," I told the Lord, "I just gave $200,000 to the Kingdom two months ago for the Now Center. Besides the money, I am *scared* to do television. I have never done television. I really don't *want* to do television!"

But I felt that still small voice when I would pray, telling me to trust Him and keep moving forward. In the evenings I would take that gold coin down to the ocean and pray. I prayed in the Spirit and paced that beach until I felt peace. But as soon as I started to head back up to the beach house, my mind would scream, *What are you thinking?! This is crazy!* So I would turn around, go back down to the beach, get that coin out and begin praying again. This went on for about two weeks, and finally, the day before we left Hawaii, I felt peace about signing the broadcast contract. I had *no idea* where the money would come from, but I knew that God would bring it in somehow. So when we got home, we signed the contract, bought the $30,000 database we needed, and set the employees and television equipment in place to launch the broadcast.

About that time, I received a call from a minister. His Christian broadcast talked about the Kingdom of God, so he asked me if I would come down and be interviewed on the show. I had never heard of this particular minister before, nor had I seen his show, but I said I would be glad for the opportunity to share. He asked me if I had any product that he could offer on his show that speaks about finances. Amazingly, when the interview aired, they sold my teachings by the thousands. I couldn't believe it. In fact, the cash flow from that interview paid for a large part of that first year on television. Something else happened that I did not expect—something that illustrates just how naïve Drenda and I were at the time. It was the day my secretary called after my interview had aired on that Christian broadcast. She said a check had come in that day for the television ministry. "What?" I exclaimed, "Is that possible?" It never dawned on me that people would send money to support the television ministry. I look back on that and marvel at how little we knew, but God was showing Himself strong.

One day soon after that, a television network called and said they would like to air our own brand-new television program, and they gave me the price it would cost. We did not have the money, but we did want to be on that network. This was on a Friday, and we had to let them know on Monday. My family often prays in our attic family room when we need to make decisions or hear from God. So my wife and I called our children together and told them what we were facing, and we asked the Lord about the network and for Him to provide the money and direction for taking this step.

On Sunday morning, a man—who came to our church as a broken, impoverished alcoholic, but who was now a born-again, successful businessman—walked up and said that he felt the Lord ask him to give the television ministry $120,000 which was the exact amount needed for that new station. (I will tell you Mike and Stacy's story later in this book.) So we signed that contract on Monday!

The whole year passed, and Drenda and I ended up not having to put *any* of our own money toward television. Today, the ministry continues to grow and now requires millions of dollars every year to do what it does. Would I have been able to handle this weight any earlier in my ministry? No way! But I was diligent to face pressure after pressure and to grow to the point that it was time to occupy the vision God had given me so many years earlier.

When you are in the right season to occupy what God has shown you, you can be sure that the money will be there as well. So be sure to remember the powerful Kingdom money mysteries of *strategy* and *timing* covered in this chapter. Understanding the process brings peace, especially when you know that God is in charge and you can confidently work with Him to accomplish huge things in the earth realm together. Remember the gold coin—and remember that God knows where the money is!

> *I will give you the treasures of darkness, riches stored in secret places, so that you may know that I am the Lord, the God of Israel, who summons you by name* (Isaiah 45:3).

Chapter Four

THE MYSTERY
IS NOT A MYSTERY

Jesus spoke all these things to the crowd in parables; He did not say anything to them without using a parable. So was fulfilled what was spoken through the prophet, "I will open My mouth in parables, I will utter things hidden since the creation of the world" (Matthew 13:34-35).

WHY did Jesus speak in parables? By now, maybe you already understand and have the answer to this question. In a simple answer, it was so that the meaning, or the truths of the Kingdom, would be hidden from satan and evil people. In the Scripture quoted from Matthew above, the Bible is plain. Jesus is speaking mysteries or truths about the Kingdom that He wants to remain hidden from the enemy. It is important, however, that we realize that these mysteries are not to be mysteries to us, the children of God, but are to be understood by us so that we can walk in our Father's Kingdom with confidence and success. We will find out in this chapter that it is only because of our ability to pick up on these hidden truths that we can win and overcome the enemy; it is never in our own strength! Look at these passages:

> *When He was alone, the Twelve and the others around Him asked Him about the parables. He told them, "The **secret** of the kingdom of God has been given to you. But to those on the outside everything is said in parables so that, 'they may be ever seeing but never perceiving, and ever hearing but never understanding; otherwise they might turn and be forgiven'"* (Mark 4:10-12).

> *For whatever is hidden is meant to be disclosed, and whatever is concealed is meant to be brought out into the open. If anyone has ears to hear, let him hear* (Mark 4:22-23).

People all over the world read the Bible and only find nice little stories within it. There is no spiritual impact as they read the stories. Yet to those who have ears to hear, revelation jumps from the pages and brings understanding and light concerning the Kingdom of God. In essence, when Jesus mentioned having hears to hear, He really was not talking about our physical ears. He was talking about our spirits and our ability to pick up the voice of the Holy Spirit. We have the Storyteller within us—the Holy Spirit. When we read or hear a parable, we can pick up its meaning, but satan is blind to the meaning within the parables. Remember, satan dwells in darkness; his perception of God and God's plans is perverted. What may appear to us as obvious because we're children of God is not so obvious to satan, at least not up front.

But he will figure out that God is up to something by our words and the anointing on our lives. Remember, the anointing on our lives always increases as God moves us to engage in new territory. Satan can see that change, even though he has no idea why the anointing is increasing. Praise God, Jesus said that we have a right to know the mysteries of the Kingdom of God. The Holy Spirit works with those who have noble hearts and desire to hear in order to bring revelation and clarity to the parables and stories.

This is also why our night dreams are in story form. We usually have to interpret a dream. The spiritual meaning is not usually obvious. Again, this is for our protection and the advancement of God's agenda. Once we start to get a handle on how all this functions and train ourselves to discern the hidden mysteries of the Kingdom, we will be postured for victory.

When it comes to money, I have already stated that satan does not want you to have it. He does not care if an unbeliever worships money, but he hates a believer who is prospering within his territory, the earth realm. Remember, God does not have money—the only way God can get money to you is to give you a plan to capture or create it. Money is created by ideas in the marketplace. I shared how the life of Dan the farmer was changed when he followed the leading of the Holy Spirit, and I also shared how my life was changed by the power of the Holy Spirit too. Your life can change, too! But you must do it through divine strategies and not in your own strength.

These divine strategies may be so unusual to you that unless you are trained to follow the leading of the Holy Spirit, you may not pick up on them. For instance, how usual is it for people to catch a fish with a gold coin in its mouth? Well think about it: if you had taxes to pay and you heard in your spirit a thought that said, *Go down to the lake and catch a fish and you will find a gold coin in its mouth to pay your taxes,* what would you think? Now add to this the fact that you are a professional fisherman who has caught thousands of fish, but never one with a gold coin in its mouth. I will tell you what most Christians would do. They would discard it as foolishness and never act on it.

I know what you are thinking, *I would certainly act on that if I heard God say it.* Well I submit this to you then. Have you ever walked through a store and saw something on the shelf that you had thought of years earlier? Have you ever thought of an invention, but never pursued it? Have you ever thought of starting your own business, but never took any steps toward doing so? I think you will have to agree that the answer is *yes*, so you can see that you may have been hearing answers all along, but never recognized them as such.

We must become good at hearing and *acting* on these unique and sometimes strange strategies that the Holy Spirit is going to bring to us to use against the enemy. I mentioned earlier how I started my own business helping people get out of debt. Think about that for a minute. I was in serious debt at the time. I had done everything wrong with money that someone could do wrong. I felt like such a failure, but God spoke to me saying that I should start a company helping people get out of debt! Actually, God spoke to Drenda first.

One night, Drenda stayed up to pray about our dire situation. She ran upstairs to our bedroom and woke me up and said, "God just spoke to me and told me that we are going to help people get out of debt and help them with their marriages." My response was to mumble sarcastically, "I wish He would show me first." I then turned over and drifted back into a miserable sleep. That idea was just crazy—I mean, it was just ridiculous. I knew nothing about computers or how to run a business. Surely, this could not be God. But the desire kept increasing, and God spoke to me in a dream one night that it was indeed His voice and to move on it.

Now you must know that I knew nothing about running a business and was not the sharpest knife in the drawer, so to speak. I had graduated with only one guy lower than me in my high school graduating class. (Hey, at least I graduated!) I was not administrative and did not really like numbers. I did have *some* experience selling life insurance, but to develop a company that would help people get out of debt? First of all, I would have loved to know how to do that for myself, let alone start a company to help others do that. With some fear, I left the life insurance company and started my own company. I attracted other representatives who also needed answers in their own financial lives. Together, we began to grow a company.

The company *did* grow and actually produced enough income to get us completely out of debt. In fact, I received a phone call from the president of one of our vendors one day that went something like this: "Gary, just wanted to let you know that your office has become our number one office out of 5,000 offices worldwide. Congratulations." *What?* I couldn't believe it. I was not even watching the numbers, but God loves to take the weak and show Himself strong in their lives. The area where satan thought he had me defeated now became my strength, and God certainly gets all the glory.

People now call me a financial expert. Whenever I hear that I laugh a little bit inside. Everything I have accomplished is simply because of the Kingdom of God in me. But it all started with my ability to hear the plan, and more importantly, to act on it, no matter how foolish it sounded. So how do we hear these divine mysteries and strategies? Before I share with you how to tap into these mysteries, let me tell you the story of a man who attended one of my conferences and did just that.

Chris came to my conference because he needed answers. Chris was a new believer who was still trying to put the pieces together from the many mistakes and failures he had experienced up to that time. It seems that Chris was in business with a partner, and the partner was taking money that Chris did not know about. We would call that embezzlement. Well, the business failed, and Chris was bitter at his partner for stealing from him. Chris' fourth marriage was also failing. Although he was only in his early 40s, life had not gone well for him.

One night, Chris just decided to end it all. He drove down to a gas station with his loaded pistol at about 3 A.M., planning to kill himself. As he sat there for a moment, his cell phone rang. He saw that it was his thieving business partner and had no interest in talking to him. But the cell phone kept ringing again and again. Finally on the 11th ring, he answered it.

The first words out of his partners mouth were, "Where are you, and what are you doing?" Chris told him that he was going to end it all, but his partner told him to stay put and he would be right there. Chris did not know this, but his partner had just given his heart to the Lord and had felt such an urgency to call Chris at that very moment. To make a long story short, the business partner led him to the Lord that night, and everything changed for Chris. Now he wanted his marriage to work, and he wanted to start over.

Although now a believer, Chris still had no income source since his business had closed down. He had no idea what he was going to do. He came to the first night of my financial conference, and he heard me teaching about letting the Holy Spirit lead you into strange tactics and new directions. Chris went home and thought about it. He really did not have any talent that was marketable. But as he kept praying, he had a strange thought. He loved to cook, and he made a mean cheesecake. This was not just any cheesecake, but a healthy one, made with healthy ingredients. He had tried the local health food store's cheesecake before and thought it fell far short of his. So he had an idea to bake a cheese-cake and take it down to the health food store and see if they would be open to selling it. When he got to the store, he explained what he wanted to do, and they agreed to taste it. They carried it to the back room, and Chris waited impatiently for their response.

They came back and said that the CEO from California just hap-pened to be in the Florida location that day and had loved the cheese-cake. This CEO wanted to talk to him further. The CEO admitted that the cheesecake was the best cheesecake he had ever had and asked Chris what else he baked. Chris confidently said, "Anything you want." The CEO asked Chris to come back the next day to discuss a contract.

That evening Chris came to the second session of my conference and asked for prayer, telling me some of the story. All I really understood at that point was that Chris said he had a multi-million dollar contract he wanted me to pray with him about. The third night of the conference, Chris came running up to the front and told me that he had just signed a huge contract with the health food chain to supply them with baked goods. Then surprisingly, on the last night of the conference the CEO himself came to our session. At the end he came forward and gave his life to God and was baptized with the Holy Spirit! What a story!

Two weeks later, I received a letter in the mail from the CEO thanking me for praying with him and a note saying that he had given Faith Life Now Ministries 10 percent of his stock in the health food chain. The CEO said he felt that he wanted his business to partner with the Kingdom of God, and felt this was the best way to do it. Such a simple idea literally changed not only Chris's life, but this CEO's life, as well.

This story is just an example of how the Holy Spirit will give us mysteries to walk out and bring us to opportunities that boggle our minds. When I left Florida, Chris asked me to pray with him about one more thing. He now needed a building to house his bakery. I assured him that God would provide, just as he had provided the contract.

I get emails everyday from desperate people who want God to help them with their finances. The mistake they make is they look in all the wrong places. Most of them assume that God is going to show up somewhere outside of their own situation, and that's where they will find their help. They may be hoping that someone gives them money or that their church will pay the rent for them or possibly that they will win the lottery. Having this attitude will not produce the results they are looking for because they need to look to the Kingdom of God for their answer—*and the Kingdom of God is in them*. Jesus said, "*The kingdom of God does not come with your careful observation nor will people say, 'Here it is,' or 'There it is,' because the kingdom of God is in you"* (Luke 17:20-21).

Let me say it again, the Kingdom of God is in you. Your answer, the direction you so desperately need, is already there in you. Another handout is not your answer. Once it is gone, you will face the same circumstances again. Instead, you need a whole new way of living, a new future with long-term financial stability. Second Peter 1:3 says, *"His divine power has given us everything we need for life and godliness* [or righteousness]...." You already have all things that pertain to life. God gave you all that you need to walk out life with success when He gave you the Kingdom.

In our natural minds, we really do not know how to change our lives ourselves. We will lean on our past experiences for our decision making when all along we really do not want our future to look like our past. When we are looking to move forward, we can lock ourselves into the same limitations we now live in if we base our decisions upon what we have already experienced. What we need are new, unbiased ideas and directions to take our lives to places we have never been before. Those places are mysteries to us, but not to God. Just as the Holy Spirit brings revelation and unlocks how the Kingdom of God works to us, He also unlocks our potential by revealing new and exciting things about our lives and the direction we should take.

So in review, Jesus spoke in mysteries, parables that were to be open to us as God's people, but hidden from the enemy. We will be looking at several of those parables in the rest of this book. Having confidence and knowledge of the Kingdom of God is exciting and so needed. However, the other side of the coin is that we need to know how to apply these principles to our everyday lives. There are mysteries we are to discover concerning our created destiny that, just like a parable, have been hidden from us until we are mature enough to handle them and not give them away to the enemy too soon.

We must know also that we are in a real battleground, and our ability to prosper in the midst of and in spite of our enemy will be determined by our ability to stay in tune with the Holy Spirit. He will reveal things to us we do not know and direct us to places we have never seen or thought of before. We also need to always have an attitude of alertness, knowing that our enemy prowls around like a lion seeking someone whom he may devour (see 1 Pet. 5:8). We will fail if we depend on the natural thought processes, but we can win if we allow the Holy Spirit to give us the hidden plan of action or strategy in any situation. Although we sometimes find ourselves facing what may appear as impossible circumstances, our lives are destined to be full of tales of victory and narrow escapes.

> *In Damascus the governor under King Aretas had the city of the Damascenes guarded in order to arrest me. But I was lowered in a basket from a window in the wall and **slipped through his hands** (2 Corinthians 11:32-33 emphasis added).*

It is true that our own "Book of Acts" is being written even now. If we picked it up, we should find passages just like this one about *us*. In Paul's story, we can see that the plan against Paul was discovered. When it looked like there was no way out, a way of escape was found. And the conclusion is the line I really like—Paul slipped through their hands. Our stories will be the same! There is not a more exciting way to live. But it does take some training and a lot of courage. With God, we are all up to the challenge. So let's go a step further now.

How do we tap into these mysteries for our lives? The Bible does not tell us where to live, or who to marry, or when to buy or sell a home—or does it?

||||||||||||||||||||||||||||||||||||||||||||||||||||||||||||||||||||||||||||||||||||||||||||||||||||

Chapter Five

THE MYSTERY OF VISIONS AND DREAMS

THE anointing was strong as we worshiped and praised the Lord. Our new little congregation of about 25 people had all gathered at the local Christian radio station. This station had graciously let us use a room once a week, free of charge. I was scared spitless—imagine me *a pastor*. I could not get my head around it. But I could vividly remember a few months back at my local church when the Spirit of the Lord came on me so strong I could scarcely stand, and I heard that call to start a church and to pastor God's people. It seemed there were so many more qualified people to do so. But as I stood there that night, I suddenly remembered an event that had happened 20 years ago; it was a night that had a profound effect on me and altered the plans I had for my life—I had a glimpse of my destiny!

When I was 18, I was like most kids—I hated school, loved to be outdoors hunting and fishing rather than doing chores, and was basically still trying to figure life out. But I always had a strong desire for the things of God. Even though I was not the most diligent in my class with my 1.3 GPA, I really was a good kid. I didn't party or drink, but loved to be by myself in the outdoors. My dream in life at that time was to someday be a forest ranger and live in the mountains. I was extremely shy, always sitting in the back row in my classes. One day as I was walking down a hall to my class, one of my teachers passed me and heard me talking to a friend. She stopped in her tracks, turned around and said, "You *can* talk!" It was not that I did not like people—my family always had a lot of people around—I just did not like speaking in front of people.

It seemed we always had a party going on at our house. My dad owned two pizza shops, and my brother, two sisters, and I all worked there. We loved getting to see everyone in our small town. For some reason, I was not shy in the pizza shop. I enjoyed being around the adults more than the high school students of my own age. Our lives consisted of football games where I played tackle and linebacker, my sisters cheered, and my dad ran the clock. We always had big parties at our house after the game. But I would usually sneak off to my bedroom by myself instead of hanging out with all the guests. We had a big pond in front of our house, and my dad put up lights around it and we would play ice hockey until the early hours of the morning with friends. My mom came from a big family that was very close, so we were always doing something with our cousins, and life was really good. It truly was a great way to grow up. I was raised in a Christian home, and one summer I gave my heart to the Lord at a vacation Bible school being held up the street from my house. From that moment on, I always had a heart for God.

The church I went to, however, was more on the religious side, and I was hungry for the deeper things of God. I was convinced that life in Christ should be just as exciting as it was for the early Church, as recorded in the Books of Acts. Although I saw no evidence of this in the churches I knew of, I just felt there had to be more than what I saw out there. One day, an evangelist came by the pizza shop and told me he was holding a revival at the local Methodist church and invited me to come. I had heard of this little church. A few of my friends went there, so I decided to go.

The Spirit of God was strong at the little revival, and I committed my life to the Lord in a new way. I started attending church there, and while there I noticed a few of the women talking about miracles, saying that they were still for today. They also mentioned something called the Baptism of the Holy Spirit, something that I had never heard about. So I started talking to them about the Lord, and they asked me to come out to their weekly morning Bible study. Since I worked at the pizza shop at night, I said I could come out. It was in that Bible study that I first became aware of the gifts of the Holy Spirit and the power of God. They told me all about this Baptism in the Holy Spirit and invited me to attend a big citywide meeting being held by a group called "Women Aglow."

It was during that meeting that I encountered the Holy Spirit in a real and personal way. During the meeting, a woman taught about the power of God and receiving the Baptism of the Holy Spirit. She then asked people to come forward if they were interested in receiving this Baptism. When they laid their hands on me, I immediately began to pray in tongues, and the anointing of God came on me. I was thrilled. I now knew that the Book of Acts had not ended. God desired to do the same things in my generation.

During this time, I had become the youth leader in the Methodist church I was attending. We had about 15 kids who would come out on Sunday nights for fellowship and a small Bible study. I could not wait to tell them what happened to me. At the time, I did not realize there was a controversy raging over the Baptism in the Holy Spirit in the churches, and I never dreamed my pastor would have any problem with it. I would later find out that would not be the case. So on that next Sunday night, the youth gathered in the basement, and I began to share with them what had happened to me. I simply told them to bow their heads and to just ask for the baptism in the Holy Spirit if they wanted to receive it. I really had no idea what I was doing, but was just copying some of the things I had heard at the Women Aglow meeting. We all bowed our heads and prayed. I began to hear weeping, then laughter. I looked up to find about half of the kids there shaking, crying, and above everything else, praying in tongues! Wow! Another thing I noticed was that they seemed to be glowing.

About this time, the pastor who was sitting next to me the entire time tapped me on the shoulder and motioned for me to step into the next room for a minute. He looked me in the eye and said, "This is of the devil." I was crushed by his comment. I really could not see how it was of the devil. I had not touched them, coached them, or encouraged any of the manifestations we observed. But he made it clear that I would have to resign as the youth leader, as well. Well, you can imagine how devastated I was. All my friends now went to that church. I did not really know what to do. The following Sunday, however, left no room in my mind as to what I would have to do.

That Sunday, I sat in the back with the youth. Remember, I was only a youth myself, being 19 years of age. I was in the doghouse with the pastor, and I did not know how to proceed with God. In the Methodist church I was attending, we always said the Lord's Prayer and had a quiet moment of meditation. It was during this quiet moment of meditation that it happened. The church was completely silent and everyone had their heads bowed.

That was when I felt someone tapping me on the shoulder. I was sitting on the aisle on the left side of the church when someone began tapping me on my right shoulder. This person was obviously standing in the aisle. I was shocked! Someone was actually standing and moving around during this time of meditation, the most holy moment during the entire service? I looked up to see one of the youth who had just received this Baptism of the Holy Spirit the week before. He simply said, "Let's go." I had no idea what he was talking about. I remember thinking, *Let's go where?* But I knew that things were not going to stay calm much longer because he was glowing just like he had when he received the Baptism of the Holy Spirit a week earlier.

He then went on to explain to me in hushed tones that his mother was sick and that he wanted to go and pray for her. I figured that he was going to walk up to the front where his mother was sitting on the second row and quietly pray for her. I would simply just tell the church what he was doing. I could do that. But that is not how it happened. Instead, he walked up to where his mother was and picked her up and carried her to the front of the church, right in front of the pastor, who was seated in one of those ornate throne-like chairs. There my friend began praying for his mother in tongues as loud as he could!

At that moment, the quiet moment of meditation was over, and now everyone was looking at me. All of a sudden I realized why he had wanted me to come along. He had planned to pray in tongues all along, and he also knew that no one there would understand what was going on. I was the one who had led him in the Baptism of the Holy Spirit, and he figured that I could explain the same to the congregation. A little shaken by being thrust into the situation, I think I just explained that she was sick and he was praying for her in tongues, which I assured them was in the Bible. I felt it was not time for a long sermon when the pastor was now staring at both of us.

Well, the bottom line was that she was healed! She had been facing major back surgery and the doctors wanted to fuse five of her vertebrae together—but now she stood completely healed. The church was in shock by what had taken place, yet they eventually saw that she had been healed. Although I loved that church and its people, I knew it was time for me and my small group of disciples to move on to a new church where the power of the Holy Spirit was a normal part of church life.

As you can see, receiving the Baptism of the Holy Spirit was a major turning point in my life. Through the years, I have also learned that the Holy Spirit is one of the keys to walking in discernment and walking out mysteries. It radically changed my life in so many ways that it would take another book to describe them all. As I continue, however, you will see how this baptism will help you to walk out the mysteries of the Kingdom when you don't know what to do. Before I go there, I want to give you yet another personal example from my life illustrating how the Holy Spirit will reveal the mysteries of your own created purpose. Without the ability to walk by the Spirit, you would be doomed to walk in dull religion.

It was shortly after receiving the Baptism of the Holy Spirit that I had my next major experience with God. I had been invited by some friends, not all of whom were believers, to celebrate my birthday. They had prepared a great meal. I remember that steak was served because when I was about to take my first bite that night, and my fork was half-way between the plate and my mouth, the Spirit of God came on me in a very strong way. It was so strong that my fork stopped in midair. I did not know what to do. I was overcome by His presence and just sat there for a moment trying to decide what to do. Everyone stopped and looked at me. Casually, I simply asked if I could be excused. Just behind me was a screen door that went out to the back yard. I figured I would go out there for a minute to sort things out.

As I slipped out the door, the anointing increased even further, and I fell to the ground. I now saw a vision before me. Whether it was an actual open vision or a picture from up out of my spirit, I do not know. But I saw a picture of myself with a Bible in my hand teaching people who sat in folding chairs. A voice, which I knew was the voice of the Lord, said, "You are called to preach My Word." This phrase was repeated three times. I also noticed there were windows in the room where I was teaching and that it was night. Just as suddenly as the anointing came on me, it lifted. I made my way back into the house and declared that I had just been called to preach God's Word. My little group of friends were polite, but must have thought I was nuts.

Years later, standing there worshiping that evening in the radio station, I noticed that the scene before me was the *exact scene* I had seen on that birthday night 20 years earlier. The people were sitting in folding chairs. The windows were dark as it was night outside. And the crowd and surroundings matched the crowd that I had seen 20 years earlier. I was comforted as I thought about the huge task that lay before me as a new pastor. Because of the revealed mystery 20 years earlier, I had successfully traveled a path that brought me to that exact intersection of time. Everything would be OK. I was right where God wanted me to be.

So let me say right here that we can war, fighting through hard times, with those revelations and mysteries. Through those earlier years, with just that one glimpse into my future, I made it. That vision spoke to me all those years every time I had to make a decision or persevere through some difficulties. Habakkuk 2:3 says,

> For the revelation awaits an appointed time; it speaks of the end and will not prove false. Though it linger, wait for it; it will certainly come and will not delay.

As we hold on to these visions and dreams that the Holy Spirit gives us, we can stand on them. They will hold us steady as we launch into the unchartered and what may appear to us as unstable and possibly even dangerous territory. I have a drawer of mementos in my office that represent the times when I heard God speak to me. I have had to hold on to His voice during some of the hard times that were required in my obedience. Now they represent a victory so grand that I stand back in amazement. But at the time there was pressure and fear.

As I said in an earlier chapter, God reveals glimpses of our future, just enough to get us started down the right path. In my case, the call to preach led me to go to college, if you can imagine that—me, with my 1.3 GPA in high school, tackling college! That is all I could have handled at that moment. God could not have given me the whole plan at that moment in my life because I about fainted at just the prospect of going back to school. But I did not need to know the future at that moment either. I just needed to say *yes* to that direction and be obedient to it. Going to Oral Roberts University was hard—very hard—but it set my direction, and I was faithful to walk it out. But it was the hardest thing I had ever done at that point in my life. In fact, in my first year of college, I had to write a paper, and when I got it back it had a big red F on the front with the following sentence: "Is it possible that you even went to high school?" I could have answered that question with, "Yes, I was there in body, but that was about all."

Again, God does not show us the complete picture of our destiny when we are not yet able to possess it. Or sometimes there are other variables as to the season or place where our destiny will be fulfilled that we have not come to yet. So the season may not be right for us. But God will give us all we need to know to prepare us and move us toward His created destiny (place of occupation) for our lives. In my case, I knew that I was called to preach, but that was it. I had no idea how that would come to pass. I did not feel any draw toward working in a church or any other typical ministry vocation when I left for college. But the call did set my path, and all I could do was walk out what I knew.

Once we give our lives to God, He begins to train us for our destiny. He leads us and trains us for that intersection of time where everything comes together and our destiny is evident not only to us, but also to the leaders who mentor us. Learning how to walk out the Kingdom and how to walk out the mysteries of our lives is vital to our eventual success, and I trust this book is helping you understand the process. For me, that training came in a method that caught me totally by surprise.

Although I had been called to preach God's Word when I was 19 years of age, as I neared the end of my college days, it seemed I came to a dead-end street. Again, I had no leading or desire to pursue ministry in the traditional sense. So I was a little confused as to what God would have me do. I was working in a floors and windows shop installing mini-blinds. I overheard my boss talking to his insurance agent about some things one day, and something in me just leaped. I wanted to learn about finances. I found the conversation extremely interesting. Several months later, I received a phone call from a man who was offering me a position in the financial field selling insurance and investments. Although I had never applied for the job, a friend of mine gave him my name as someone who was looking for some work. I was drawn to it and found my heart moved by it, but I was still confused. How did this fit with the call of God on my life?

During this same time I met the love of my life, Drenda. And on this particular weekend, I was headed to Georgia to ask her father for her hand in marriage, and we were planning to attend her home church, as well. It was during that Sunday service at her home church that a lady I had never seen before walked up to me and said that she had a word from the Lord for me and asked if she could share it? Well, this was a little new to me, but I encouraged her to go ahead and share it. She then simply stated, "You are looking at a job that does not make sense to you. The Lord has shown me ten attributes of the job you are looking at." She then listed them one by one. She concluded her remarks by saying, "You are to take the job." Wow; she had described the job that had been offered to me completely. I now knew that the Lord had opened that job for me, and I was at peace with it, so I took the job.

I stayed in that job for nine years. Living on commissions, talking to people on a non-stop basis, was the hardest thing I had ever done, and I wanted to quit a million times. You remember how shy I was in high school? Now God put me in a place that forced me to walk outside my comfort zone on a daily basis. Fear was my constant companion, but my leadership skills and my ability to persevere were being developed—and these were exactly the skills I would need to pastor a growing church. But learning those skills caused me to die a thousand deaths a day as I laid my life down and submitted my will to His. Growth can be uncomfortable. Every time I wanted to quit, I would be reminded of that prophecy, and I stayed steady.

So many people quit and give up when they need to persevere and learn what there is to learn in the places they find themselves. But without the revelation, without the "ears that hear," people have nothing to hang on to when they step out. Most think that following God will be easy, but we need to remember that we have an adversary who will not let us just walk into his domain and take what we want. Although we have all authority, he will challenge it over and over again. Every successful person must be trained. As Hebrews 12:7-8 says,

> *Endure hardship as discipline; God is treating you as sons.*
> *For what son is not disciplined by his Father? If you are not*
> *disciplined (and everyone undergoes discipline), then you*
> *are illegitimate children and not true sons.*

The word *hardship* is referring to the hardship of obedience, the price of obedience. It was what I learned during those years of hardship that gave me the understanding to pastor God's people. So many people get a glimpse of their destiny, jump, and fail to understand the process that the Holy Spirit uses to train us and mold us for our assignment. That is why we have pastors and elders who are to agree with us and confirm that we are mature enough to embrace our destiny. They have watched our lives and know whether or not it is time to step out. But the bottom line is that we must walk each day out, paying close attention to the direction and details for that day.

Once, when pastoring seemed hard and I was overcome with many decisions, I had a dream. In the dream I was standing on a perfectly straight road. Its black pavement stretched before me into the horizon as far as I could see. A voice said to walk down the road. So I started walking. Suddenly barriers began to appear. You know those concrete barriers that construction crews use when they are working on the freeway? Well, one would appear and lay across one of the lanes of the highway. As I walked, more and more would appear. But it was really no trouble to continue walking since I could easily just walk around the barriers in the other lane. Then someone came up behind me and blindfolded me with a cloth. Now I could see nothing. I asked, "How can I walk down the road without seeing?" The voice said that I would not be able to unless I allowed God's Spirit to lead me around the road blocks I could not see. Remember, nothing is hidden from the Lord. He sees everything, even what the enemy is trying to do. He will get us down the road as we listen and move with Him.

This is the key. We must allow God to lead us to the place in which we were created to live. As I mentioned in a previous chapter, our destiny is really a place, a place of occupation. In reality, God has prepared a place for each of us to occupy and to take for the Kingdom of God. All of the training on the road to that place is just that—training. Everyone has a place of occupation they are given to take and to hold under God's government. But again, that place is a mystery to us, and we must learn how to walk out the Kingdom principles before we get there. The war in the earth realm is really a war in which we overcome with divine strategy and timing, a revelation of mysteries, direction, and gifting that we walk out. But here is the great news. We have mighty weapons that help us walk in the light, knowing exactly what we should do and how to do it. We do not walk as the world does, stumbling through life in the dark, hoping things will work out.

The title of this book talks about the money mysteries, and you may think that I should be talking more about money by now. But what you need to know and what I found out is that *money is tied very closely to your destiny and assignment in the Kingdom.* These same principles

I am covering now will have tremendous impact on your finances, because finances are essential for you to be effective in occupying your destiny and your assignment. But as I said before, no one is just going to hand you the money needed for your assignment. You will have to capture it with a divine strategy and literally take it from the dominion of the enemy! I know, you're thinking this sounds like a James Bond movie plot. Oh no, it is much better than that! In a James Bond movie, he always comes out on top, and so will you. But also like a James Bond movie, many times it will look like it is over and there is no way out. However, there is something I have learned and tested on the road to my destiny. You have a super weapon that the enemy hates. In fact he has tried to stop Christians from knowing about this weapon by telling them it does not even exist.

> *We do, however, speak a message of wisdom among the mature, but not the wisdom of this age or of the rulers of this age, who are coming to nothing. No, we speak of God's secret wisdom, a wisdom that has been hidden and that God destined for our glory before time began. None of the rulers of this age understood it, for if they had, they would not have crucified the Lord of glory. However, as it is written: "**No eye has seen, no ear has heard, no mind has conceived what God has prepared for those who love Him,**" but God has revealed it to us by His Spirit. The Spirit searches all things, even the deep things of God. For who among men knows the thoughts of a man except the man's spirit within him? In the same way, no one knows the thoughts of God except the Spirit of God. We have not received the spirit of the world but the Spirit who is from God, that we may understand what God has freely given us. This is what we speak, not in words taught us by human wisdom but in words taught by the Spirit, expressing spiritual truths in spiritual words. The man without the Spirit*

does not accept the things that come from the Spirit of God, for they are foolishness to him, and he cannot understand them, because they are spiritually discerned. The spiritual man makes judgments about all things, but he himself is not subject to any man's judgment: For who has known the mind of the Lord that he may instruct Him? But we have the mind of Christ (1 Corinthians 2:6-16).

We read this Scripture back in Chapter 3, but now I want to point out the process that is revealed in that passage whereby we walk with victory through the valley of the shadow of death. The battle plan is all here in this Scripture! I have already pointed out a key principle recorded here: satan will change tactics if he can pick up on the plan of God. So remember, there is wisdom in how we handle the revelations God gives us regarding our assignments. It is also mandatory that we pay attention to the timing and details of what the Lord shows us. In many, if not in *every* confrontation we encounter, understanding timing and revelation will be the difference between victory and defeat.

When I say revelation, I am speaking of our super weapon—light! The Bible is very clear when it says that we formerly lived in the kingdom of darkness. That kingdom is where satan dwells, in darkness. We all grew up there. But the Bible says in Isaiah 9 that the people who walked in darkness saw a great light. John 1:4 says, *"In Him was life, and that life was the light of men."* As believers we now live in the Kingdom of light, and we can walk without stumbling around.

To illustrate what this new ability looks like, imagine that you are walking through a room that is completely black. The room is littered with furniture and things thrown all over the floor. With every step you stumble, and with nothing to hold on to, you fall to the ground. You start to crawl, feeling your way around very slowly. But all of a sudden the lights come on and you can clearly see. How hard would it then be to walk or even run through that room? Not hard at all. In fact, it would be so easy that anyone could do it—as long as the lights were on.

So here is our advantage, our super weapon: we have access to what God sees and what He thinks! And we know that all things are laid bare to Him. *There is no darkness.* So when Peter asked Jesus about those taxes, God knew exactly where that gold coin was. When Jesus told Peter to cast out his net to catch fish, He told him exactly where to throw it: out into the deep water. Think about what I have just said. If God sees everything, then He also sees every snare and strategy that the devil is setting up to harm us, and only He can lead us around the snares.

Jesus mentions this ability to see in the darkness in the Lord's Prayer: *"And lead us not into temptation, but deliver us from the evil one"* (Matt. 6:13). As we pray and follow God, He will warn us of things we cannot see. We can know of the schemes and snares the enemy is trying to set for us that we do not yet see. This same ability is meant not only to warn us, but also to lead us into victory.

Let's take some time now to look at that Scripture in First Corinthians a little closer.

> However, as it is written, "No eye has seen, no ear has heard, no mind has conceived what God has prepared for those who love Him" but God has revealed it to us by His Spirit... (1 Corinthians 2:9-10).

Although you most likely have heard this Scripture read at a funeral, it is for the living, not the dead. Here is the simple truth behind this Scripture—you have access to things you do not know, things you have never heard, and things you have never even thought of. We are not limited to our own past or even present ability when it comes to our future or our strategy against the devil. Think about how valuable that type of information would be. So even though the enemy thinks he has you figured out and boxed in a corner, God simply drops new pictures, thoughts, and direction into your situation that catch the enemy off guard. And *bam*, you come out on top.

For instance, you may need greater income, but have no experience and don't know where to turn. God's Spirit in you has the answer and can show you new concepts and how to start a business that you would have never thought of before. Or you may not know if you should sell your house now or wait to get the best price. God has that answer, too. The list of questions in your life is of course endless. The bottom line is that, without this information, you are subject to making wrong decisions and falling into the enemy's trap. But better than just avoiding unseen pitfalls, having access to the mind of Christ turns what the devil had devised for evil into a major opportunity that God wants you to win.

Basically, success in life is really nothing more than making a series of right decisions—the right person to marry, the right subject to study in college, the right job to take, and so forth. What if I told you that this weapon gives you the ability to make the right decision *every time?* "Impossible!" you may say. Ah, but it is right here in the Bible. *"The spiritual man makes judgments about all things…"* (1 Cor. 2:15). With God, it is possible to make right decisions every time. You do not have to start and stop, wasting valuable time. You can keep moving forward with success! You can do that because of what verse 16 of the same chapter reveals. *"…But we have the mind of Christ"* (1 Cor. 2:16).

This Scripture essentially says that we have access to the thoughts of God. But how does that work? How do we tap into that? The mystery we are about to uncover in the next chapter causes every demon in hell to shudder!

‖‖‖

Chapter Six

THE MYSTERY OF PRAYING IN THE SPIRIT

I was worshiping one morning in church when the Holy Spirit spoke to me and said that someone there had lost a piece of jewelry. Our church was still small, about 150 members at the time. So I told the congregation what the Lord had said to me and asked if someone had lost some jewelry. I was surprised when my daughter Amy raised her hand. Since it was Amy, I simply told her that I would talk to her about it after church. When we sat down to lunch, I asked Amy about the jewelry she was missing. She reached into her pocket and pulled out a pearl drop earring and said that she had wanted to wear those pearl earrings that morning, but could not find the other one, although she had checked everywhere. At the time Amy was about 12 years old, and those earrings were very special to her. Amazingly, God had shown me a picture of a pearl drop earring during worship and also where it was. I was excited to tell Amy that the Lord had shown me where the earring was—in the television cabinet at home. When we got home, Amy and I went to the television cabinet and looked through it, but could not find the earring there. Later in the afternoon, as I was sitting at my desk, I kept thinking about that television cabinet. Finally, I called out and said, "Amy, I know what I saw, and I am sure that the earring has to be there. We just need to check it again." So we went back to the television cabinet, and this time we took the television and everything out of it. There in the very back, behind the television, we found the lost pearl drop earring.

We rejoiced that we had it back, and I was so thankful that I was able to demonstrate to my daughter how the Kingdom operates. I had tapped into our secret weapon to discover the mystery of where the earring was hidden. God cares about everything, including a little girl's earring. But He was using that moment to teach me and reaffirm how He will help me with the things I do not know. It is through the use of the Church's secret weapon—praying in the Spirit. As we follow the leading of the Spirit of God and pray in the Spirit, we can walk in victory and get things done that previously seemed impossible. Drenda and I have done everything we have done by using this principle. Let me give you another example from our lives.

Drenda and I lived in a small farmhouse for a number of years. And as I told you, those years were hard years, before I learned how the Kingdom of God operates. Once we plugged into the Kingdom and got completely out of debt, we began saving money to build a house. We had about $100,000 in the bank, but we were just waiting to save more money before we really began to look for land. During this time, we also began to pastor our church and things got really busy for us. We dreamed of having our own home, and we sowed, prayed, and believed God that at the right time He would show us what to do. Here is where praying in the Spirit helps us, when we do not know what to do. As we were praying about our new home, we felt impressed to do a marriage conference as a church outreach, but we felt led to pay for it out of our own pockets instead of the church paying for it. In so doing, we believed that God would show us what to do about buying the land or house that we needed.

We had gone out a few times looking at homes and land, but found out very quickly that we were too busy to do the searching that was needed. We knew that God could help us and do it much more quickly than we could do ourselves. We were basically just looking for land. We did not have enough money yet saved to buy a home, but we thought if we could buy land then we could save more money and begin the building process to pay for the house as we built it. We figured it would take us about two years or so to build our home that way, but it would be debt free when it was finished. So we sowed for our land during that marriage conference, knowing that God could do what we could not.

During the week of the conference, a member of my church walked up to me and said he had discovered the most beautiful land he had ever seen. It was 55 acres of rolling land, with about 20 acres of woods and 10 acres of wetlands on it. He then went on to say that he loved it, but it was too expensive for him, and he believed it was really supposed to be my land. I asked him where it was located, and he gave me the address. We were so busy during the week of the conference that I did not really have time to think much about the land, but we decided to at least drive out and look at it. When I saw it, it was everything I was looking for, and we almost had all the money in the bank to pay cash for it! We were short just a few thousand dollars.

I called the real estate agent and told him I was tied up that week doing a conference and asked him if he would hold it for me until the next week when I could really consider it. He agreed to hold it for me until the Monday after the conference. To make a long story short, we bought that land. This is an example of how the Lord works for us when we work with the Kingdom of God; He directs our path in every situation. And wouldn't you know, right smack in the middle of the land we found the name "Gary" carved into a huge oak tree! My wife joked and said it was still smoking from where God carved it. We loved our new land and we would have never found it by ourselves. But by praying in the Spirit and following the plan God laid out for us and sowing where God said to sow, God led us to the perfect land that fit our budget.

At that time I had no plans to build the house that year. We had purchased the land in March, but I knew that I needed time to get more money together to begin the building process. However, one day as I was sitting in our living room I had an open vision, like a curtain being pulled back. I saw a window into the spirit realm. Suddenly, I saw the farmhouse in which I sat, completely empty. The living room and the dining room suddenly were vacant. Then, just as suddenly, that curtain closed and I was back in my furnished home. Instantly, I knew that we were to move and move *now*. We scurried to design the house plans and secure a builder during that summer. We broke ground in October. Without going through the details, we walked out the building process with great excitement.

In March of the following year, we received a call from the landlord who owned the farmhouse we rented. He informed us that he had sold the farm and that we would need to move out in 30 days! However, our new home was not quite complete. We spoke with the new owners of our farmhouse, and they graciously gave us two more months to finish our home. We moved into our dream home on the fourth of July weekend. Even though the home was not completely finished when we moved in, it was much closer than it would have been if I had not had the vision to build quickly.

The point I am making is that if we had not heard God's Spirit, we would have missed the timing and found ourselves having to move twice instead of once. Just as God helped us find the earring, find the land we needed, and discern our building timeline, He will direct your steps as you tap into His thoughts. Wouldn't it be great if God helped you prosper this way? My friend, He *will* help you prosper in the same way.

When we pick up on His mysteries, things we do not already know, God will lead us to victory. But now, let's study the mechanics of how we actually do that. Again, it's all explained right here in First Corinthians 2.

> ..."*No eye has seen, no ear has heard, no mind has conceived what God has prepared for those who love Him" but God has revealed it to us by His Spirit. The Spirit searches all things, even the deep things of God. For who among men knows the thoughts of a man except the man's spirit within Him? In the same way no one knows the thoughts of God except the Spirit of God. We have not received the spirit of the world but the Spirit who is from God, that we may understand what God has freely given us. This is what we speak, not in words taught us by human wisdom but in words taught by the Spirit, expressing spiritual truths in spiritual words* (1 Corinthians 2:9-13).

Here, Paul was saying that we have access to the things we have not ever heard or seen or thought, just as I have been sharing with you. And he tells us how it works.

> *For who among men knows the thoughts of a man except the man's spirit within him? In the same way no one knows the thoughts of God except the Spirit of God* (1 Corinthians 2:11).

Before I cover this aspect of the Scripture, we need to first have a basic lesson in our makeup. According to First Thessalonians 5:23, we are three parts: spirit, soul, and body. Our spirit is the God part of us. Our soul is our mind, will, and emotions. Our body is the physical house for our spirit and soul. Paul was saying that our souls (mind, will, and emotions) and spirits are so closely connected that our spirits know what our thoughts are and the reverse is true, as well. So let's catch this important point, based on what Paul said: our minds can pick up thoughts from our spirit. Paul also said that God's Spirit knows God's thoughts as well. When we are born again, our spirits become one with God's Spirit giving us access to the thoughts of God. Paul stated this very fact when he said that we have received God's Spirit so that *we may know* what God has freely given us.

> We have not received the spirit of the world but the Spirit who is from God, that we may understand what God has freely given us. This is what we speak, not in words taught us by human wisdom but in words taught by the Spirit, expressing spiritual truths in spiritual words (1 Corinthians 2:12-13).

Paul went on to say that this mystery knowledge is what we speak with words that are taught us by the Spirit, not words that we would speak in our natural understanding or language. Let me clarify. Paul said we are speaking with spiritual words about things that we have not seen, heard, or thought of before. Paul said this comes from God's Spirit Himself. But when Paul said we are speaking these mysteries out with spiritual words, what did he mean by that? We can get a clue when Paul mentioned this same phrase in First Corinthians 14:14-15.

> For if I pray in a tongue, my spirit prays, but my mind is unfruitful. So what shall I do? I will pray with my spirit, but I will also pray with my mind; I will sing with my spirit, but I will also sing with my mind.

Paul was using the phrase *"pray in the spirit"* as it refers to speaking in tongues. So we can assume that Paul was referring to this same speaking in tongues when he said that we speak with words taught to us by the Spirit in First Corinthians 2.

> *For anyone who speaks in a tongue does not speak to men,
> but to God. Indeed, no one understands him; **he utters
> mysteries with his spirit** (1 Corinthians 14:2).*

Again, Paul explained that our spirits have the ability to speak out things that we have never seen, heard, or had knowledge of—or as Paul called them, mysteries. Also notice in this verse that Paul said we are praying out mysteries with *our* own spirits. We would then have to ask how something we did not know got into our spirits. That one is easy! It's by God's Spirit, who is now one with our spirits.

> *For who among men knows the thoughts of a man except
> the man's spirit within him? In the same way no one knows
> the thoughts of God except the Spirit of God* (1 Corinthians
> 2:11).

When our spirits pick up on the thoughts of God, our minds also pick up on these thoughts. When our minds pick up on the thoughts of God, we call this *revelation* or being *enlightened*. We receive light, and we can see what to do in any situation. Paul gave us further instruction in his letter to the Romans regarding how our spirits can bring light on a subject.

> *...The Spirit helps us in our weakness. We do not know
> what we ought to pray for, but the Spirit Himself intercedes
> for us with groans that words cannot express. And He who
> searches our hearts knows the mind of the Spirit, because
> the Spirit intercedes for the saints in accordance with God's
> will* (Romans 8:26-27).

Paul was saying that a person who does not know the will of God stands in a place of weakness, not knowing how to pray. I think we can all relate to this at times, when a decision can go either way and we just do not know the right way to go. First John 5:14-15 says,

This is the confidence we have in approaching God: that if we ask anything according to His will, He hears us. And if we know that He hears us—whatever we ask—we know that we have what we asked of him (1 John 5:14-15).

This Scripture is not talking about God hearing us like we hear a sound, but rather He hears us like a judge hears a case. We know that if we ask anything according to the will of God, then God hears the case, and judges it according to spiritual law. So understand this, there can be no faith until the will of God is known. That is why Paul says if we do not know the will of God, we stand in a place of weakness. But the Spirit of God will help us pray the perfect will of God for our lives when we do not know how to pray. This kind of prayer is of the Spirit, spoken with words and groans that are beyond our normal vocabulary. Again, Paul is speaking of praying in the Spirit or praying in tongues.

So let me abbreviate these thoughts. When you do not know what to do, you have access to the thoughts of God, to things you have never heard, seen, or thought before. These mysteries bubble up into our consciousness from our own spirits as we pray in tongues. Praying in tongues means allowing the Spirit of God to pray God's perfect will through our spirits. As we pray in the Spirit, God's thoughts are picked up by our minds and become known to us.

Now here is the mighty weapon in all of this. Satan does not know what we are saying, and neither do other people. But as we continue to pray in the Spirit, we can pick up on the secret plan of God for us at that moment. You see, God has His own secret messaging code in the earth realm. I just think this is so awesome, way better than a James Bond movie! Through this system of praying in the Spirit, we can always walk in the light and have daily direction that will put us ahead of the enemy every time.

So when it comes to money, we now can understand that our future must come from things we have not seen, thought of, or heard. We can assume that we are already operating in what we already know. When we need a business idea or new marketing concepts for our businesses, we can always pray in the Spirit to pick up on the direction we should go. This is what Jesus did. When He told Peter where to throw that net for that huge catch of fish in the deep water, that direction was a word of knowledge from the Spirit of God. When Jesus told Peter about the gold coin, that was also a word of knowledge from the Spirit of God.

Just as the Spirit of God knew how to take care of those situations, He also knows how to take care of yours. By the Spirit you receive mysteries regarding your situation, and you can then walk them out!

‖‖‖

Chapter Seven

THE MYSTERY
OF PARTNERSHIP

I get emails all the time from people who have discovered what I believe to be the most powerful money mystery in the Bible—the mystery of partnering with God. Can you imagine what could happen if you had God as a business partner helping you prosper? Well, the Bible says that is exactly what God wants to do. Here is an email that I received from Jim and Pam, a couple that began attending my church after seeing our television show *Faith Life Now*.

> My wife and I have been running a business out of our home for over 12 years. The business provides engineering and computer-aided design services to various companies and individuals. Over that time we've seen progress, and God has opened doors that have blessed our company and our family. However, there were still some pieces of the puzzle missing, and we would still have times when our business would be in lack. We hit one of those times in August of 2009.

As you know the banking system in our country had collapsed and along with it, the economy. Late in the summer of 2009 our business dried up, and we weren't sure how we were going to make it. God had taught us that he would provide, but we knew he wanted more for us than just barely making it. God did faithfully provide for every bill, but it was still a difficult place to be in. We were going to a mainstream denominational church in our hometown of Marysville, and we were growing increasingly frustrated. We were looking fervently for a new church. We had already been studying that God wanted us to prosper, yet it seemed unlikely that we would find a church around us that would teach that message.

I happened to turn on Channel 28 one Sunday morning and saw you and Drenda preaching and teaching the Kingdom of God and how to live in it here on earth. I was very excited but figured you were located somewhere far away. I was amazed that you were located in New Albany. Although it was a forty-five minute drive from Marysville, my wife and I started attending the Saturday night services. Over the years our company had consisted largely of me, and occasionally someone else helping me, or to put it in your words, I was a job owner not a business owner. Your teachings on having a net to harvest the wealth reinvigorated my enthusiasm for our company and got me out of a "mail box mentality." We knew that we also needed to disconnect from the world's curses and reconnect to the Kingdom of God through our faith and our attention. You taught us to be specific when using the laws of the kingdom. One morning it came up strong in me to command not only the work to come but also the personnel to come to do the work. We had been sowing and giving financially into your ministry, and when those faith-filled words were spoken, it unleashed a blessing on us that we literally couldn't contain.

The director of engineering from one of our customers called. He had a huge project that he needed help on, but he knew I was a one-horse operation at the time. He said, "It's apparent that I'm going to have to force you to hire some personnel!" I was still kind of stuck in my old vision of myself and our company, and when he said that I started going through the hiring process. From the first day of attending Faith Life Church, it took about four to five months to go from barely making the bills to having five people working for us. Our income quadrupled.

The people the Lord brought to work for us were so grateful. One of them commented that they had almost given up on finding a job. My wife was also given a business idea from the Spirit of God. We've been working on it throughout 2010 and will be launching it soon. The preliminary response to it has been very strong. Both Pam and I deeply appreciate your ministry. When we see you and Drenda up there on the stage, we can relate to you, and we see that just as you overcame, so can we.

We're excited to be a part of Faith Life Church.

God Bless,

Jim and Pam

What did Jim and Pam discover? There are millions of Christians who have the same problems that Jim and Pam had with their cash flow who do not know what to do. But Jim and Pam completely turned their business around. How? As a spiritual scientist, I always ask questions like that. Knowing that the Kingdom of God is just that, a Kingdom, I know that it operates by laws that can be learned. Those laws never change or fail. So when I see a story in the Word of God, I always ask, *How and why did that happen? How did that person receive? Or in some cases, why **didn't** they receive?* In this case, I can tell you what happened to Jim and Pam. They discovered the mystery of partnership, a key principle of God's Kingdom. Well, it is not really a mystery anymore since it is plainly in the Word of God. But the Kingdom operates in direct conflict with the mindset of this earth-cursed system of finance that we all grew up with—the one that says to run after money and, when you get it, to hold on to it. So let me show you what they discovered and what Drenda and I discovered years ago.

> *Remember this: Whoever sows sparingly will also reap sparingly, and whoever sows generously will also reap generously. Each man should give what he has decided in his heart to give, not reluctantly or under compulsion, for God loves a cheerful giver. And God is able to make all grace abound to you, so that in all things at all times, having all that you need, you will abound in every good work. As it is written: "He has scattered abroad his gifts to the poor; his righteousness endures forever." Now He who supplies seed to the sower and bread for food will also supply and increase your store of seed and will enlarge the harvest of your righteousness. You will be made rich in every way so that you can be generous on every occasion, and through us your generosity will result in thanksgiving to God (2 Corinthians 9:6-11).*

Paul is telling us that if we give toward God's purposes, we will reap a return. God will actually give us His grace, which means His anointing and power to prosper. In fact, it is God's desire that we prosper to the degree that we can be generous on every occasion. Let me say that again—prosper on every occasion! When we look at this Scripture, something should stand out to us: **God wants us to give our money away!** To most people who need money, this may feel like a big letdown. If we stopped here, we would portray God as most religious people see Him, as a hard taskmaster requiring us to sacrifice and give it all away for God. But stop! We would be missing the whole point. The Bible says that if we give, we will reap. God's grace and power will help us prosper even more than we were before we gave our money away.

> *Now He who supplies seed to the sower and bread for food will also supply and increase your store of seed and will enlarge the harvest of your righteousness. You will be made rich in every way so that you can be generous on every occasion, and through us your generosity will result in thanksgiving to God* (2 Corinthians 9:10-11).

According to this Scripture, we first need to recognize *who* gives us the seed to sow. We will see that God is the one who supplies the seed. But we must note that He also gives us bread for food. The bread is made from the seed taken out of our seed-sowing operation. But notice that God gives us the seed to *sow*. Why did He give us the seed? Paul tells us very plainly that the intent God had in giving it to us was for us to sow it! Yes, we can keep some of it to eat. This would include having money for our houses, our cars, and everything that pertains to our own lives. But the *purpose* of the seed—and let's make this very clear—is to sow.

Why would God want us to sow seed? Because He loves people, and Paul tells us that when we sow because we love God, the people whom we have helped will be thankful to God. You see, God knows that His goodness brings people to repentance (see Rom. 2:4), not to law. The Bible says He rains on the just and the unjust (see Matt. 5:45) and it is His will that every person receive His gift of salvation. He wants us to inherit His Kingdom. Since we are also the ambassadors of His Kingdom, we should be the most generous people on the earth today, demonstrating to everyone that God is good. But it takes money to be generous; that's why God wants us to have it. Paul is teaching here that if we will take God up on this offer and sow, He will actually increase our store of seed, and we will become rich in every way so that we can be generous on *every* occasion.

Now think about it. If you were able to be generous on every occasion, you would have to have *more than enough* seed to also provide the bread you need yourself. If you were truly going to be generous on every occasion, you would have to have enough funds on hand to not have to penny pinch and budget just to make it through the month. You would have to have more than enough. So you can see that this is God's desire for you.

Many of God's people have heard this before and have not seen the changes that they had hoped for when they did sow. But they missed something in the principle Paul taught, *"And now God is able to make **all grace** abound to you."* Most Christians believe that God will just bring the money to them out of nowhere, kind of like a big slot machine. You will hear me talk about this mailbox mentality throughout this entire book. The Bible does not say that God is your slot machine; it says that God will make all grace abound to *you*. The word *grace* here is referring to God's ability becoming your ability.

So what do you need ability to do? You can tap into His grace to plant, harvest, and capture wealth in the earth realm. But understand this, you are the one who will be doing the harvesting. This is with God's help, of course, but it will be you walking it out. So know this, God loves people and wants to reach them with the good news of His

Kingdom. But to do that, He needs more people who have the heart to sow and not just consume all their seed by making and eating their own bread from the seed that God gives them. Of course, as your flow of seed increases, you certainly can take seed and bake as much bread as you desire as long as the flow is flowing. This means you are continually sowing. Jim and Pam simply had a revelation of the Kingdom, the purpose of money, and their need to sow and partner with God.

So remember, when we sow toward God's purposes, we partner with God, and His grace is there to help us harvest through revealed mysteries and hidden treasures. But our willingness to sow is where it all starts. Just like a farmer, our prosperity starts when we sow our fields, not the day we harvest them.

But before you decide that you are just going to partner with God and start sowing, there are some things you need to know about sowing that I will discuss further. For instance, where do you sow and how do you go about it? All of these things have an impact on your harvest.

Drenda and I were completely out of debt when God called us to start a church from scratch. We had already discovered many of the keys of the Kingdom, keys that totally changed our lives, just like it did Jim and Pam's. As we gave more of our lives to the Kingdom of God, I observed an interesting trend. Each time we gave more, we prospered more. For instance, when we said *yes* to starting Faith Life Church and pastoring God's people, our income went up. When we said *yes* to supporting missions around the world, our income went up. When we said *yes* to building the Now Center and personally contributing $200,000 out of our own pocket to the project, our income went up. In fact, every time I have said *yes* to God when it came to giving more of my money and time to the Kingdom, my income went up.

As an example, this past fall we were raising more money to finish out some things at the Now Center. Drenda and I had already given $200,000 in the beginning stages of the project and found the years immediately following that gift to be the best financial years of our lives. We prospered at a new level in spite of the financial chaos that occurred in the economy during the financial crisis of 2008 and 2009. As we considered how much we wanted to give toward this new project, we wanted to give God a chance to help us prosper at an even higher level of income. Praying and meditating on what to give, Drenda and I decided that we would give $500,000 to the project out of our own money.

Amazingly, a month after we committed to do so, many of the companies I work with came to me and wanted to change their contracts with me. We were able to renegotiate new contracts that would pay us $691,000 more over the following three years, doing exactly the same thing we were doing. Incredible! We said, "Yes, Lord, we will be givers to your purposes in the earth realm." God's grace stepped in, and the $500,000 we wanted to give was supplied by nothing that we did. It was His grace.

We get a constant barrage of emails every year from people who discover the money mysteries of the Kingdom from our television broadcast and materials. Here are a couple stories that we recently received. My secretary sent me this note about a conversation she had with Joe and Kristi who called our office to say thanks for helping them understand the Kingdom of God. The note read:

> I just got off the phone with a couple named Joe and Kristi who were so excited about what has happened to them since they first heard your teaching on the Kingdom of God. When they first heard you, they had a car loan, a mortgage, school loans, and credit card debt of $10,000. Eighteen months later they are earning more income, they both have new jobs, they own a company that is prospering, they paid off their car loans, the mortgage has been paid off, and in one more month the

last credit card will be paid off. They will be completely debt free.

This email came in from Dorothy after attending a conference I conducted on how the Kingdom works:

> When you were here in Everett, Washington, I was fascinated by this approach you taught on giving. I asked Jesus if it was for me since I am 81 years of age and on a fixed income. I was trying to save $3,000 by July fifth so I gave it a try. I emptied my savings account and sowed it into your ministry. The good news is that all of the $3,000 came in by July fifth. I felt like a 20-year-old again, jumping up and down and praising my wonderful Lord for the mercy and love He has given me. Thank you so much for your ministry.

Here is another email I just received as I was writing this chapter:

> I wanted to tell you what God has done for me since applying to my life what I learned at Brother Gary's conference in April. I'm 19 years old and just finished up my freshman year as a business major. I have been in the lawn care business with my younger brother for about three years now. Before attending the conference, I had only been thinking about money and told myself how "I" was going to build up our business this year. God had other plans. For no real reason, several of our regular customers left us, and we were not getting any new lawns. I came to the conference very distraught. I did not even see how the business would survive this summer.

At the end of one of your sessions, you made a statement that stirred in my spirit. After wrestling with God, I decided to make Him my business partner and give half of what I make to church and missions. In two weeks my business had tripled, and it is still growing! I have never felt as spiritually satisfied, either, and I have given away more this month than I did all of last year. I really feel God has new ideas in store for me in the future. Thank you for your obedience and attentiveness to the Holy Spirit. It has truly changed my life.

What a blessed ministry you have.

Tyler

These things did not happen by accident. They were a direct result of partnership with God. I have found that many people really do not understand this aspect of the Kingdom, and that is why I have labeled it as a money mystery of the Kingdom. Using your money to help God reach people is a powerful money tool. There is yet another money mystery that works alongside the partnering with God principle that very few people have put into practice. But the ones who have heard it and understand it use it to get things done in a powerful way.

I was in a meeting in North Carolina and a pastor walked up to me and said, "I need to talk to you for a moment." He then went on to tell me that he was a pastor from Germany and that his teenage son had gotten a hold of my CDs. He told me that the son had begun to learn about partnering with God and decided to sow and release his faith for a new PlayStation 3. This pastor then told me that the next day someone who needed some work done on a temporary project called his son. He told me that his son made enough from that job to pay cash for the PlayStation 3.

He said, "I thought it was interesting that this guy offered my son that temporary job the day after he sowed for the PlayStation®3, but I did not really think that much about it. A few weeks later, my son came to me and asked me to agree with him as he was going to sow and release his faith for muscles." The pastor continued, "Well, I laughed and told him that he would have to help God with that one." The son said that he would, and they prayed and released their faith for the son's muscles. This pastor went on to say that the *very next day* a friend pulled into his driveway unannounced and said, "Hey, I was cleaning out my basement and thought maybe your son might want this old barbell set." The pastor told me he was shocked! He promptly went to his son and told him to give him those teaching CDs because he had to listen to them!

To open up this second mystery in regard to partnering with God, we will need to look into the Word of God where it is revealed in Luke 5.

> *One day as Jesus was standing by the Lake of Gennesaret, with the people crowding around Him and listening to the word of God. He saw at the water's edge two boats, left there by the fishermen who were washing their nets. He got into one of the boats, the one belonging to Simon, and asked him to put out a little from shore. Then He sat down and taught the people from the boat. When He had finished speaking, He said to Simon. "Put out into the deep water, and let down the nets for a catch." Simon answered, "Master, we've worked hard all night and haven't caught anything. But because You say so, I will let down the nets." When they had done so, they caught such a large number of fish that their nets began to break. So they signaled their partners in the other boat to come and help them, and they came and filled both boats so full they began to sink. When Simon Peter saw this, he fell at Jesus' knees and said, "Go away from me, Lord; I am a sinful man!" For he and all his companions were astonished at the catch of fish they had*

taken, and so were James and John, the sons of Zebedee, Simon's partners... (Luke 5:1-10).

What an amazing story illustrating the Kingdom and how it operates. You may say, "Yes, such an amazing story, if only things like this were possible today." But my friend, that is what I am trying to tell you—they *are* possible!

To understand any mystery, we first must look for facts that will lead us to a proper conclusion. In this story, Peter was the only one who went out with Jesus in the boat, and Peter was the one who followed Jesus' instructions about dropping the nets. Remember, James and John were washing their nets after fishing all night and catching nothing. But when Peter's nets began to break, he called out to his partners, who then came out and helped him bring the fish in. The Bible then says that both boats were so full they about sank. So let me ask a question. How much faith did *James and John* exhibit for that boatload of fish? The answer would be *none*. Peter was the one who acted on the word of the Lord. *"But because You say so, I will let down the nets."* So if that is the case, then why did James and John's boat catch *the same exact haul of fish* that Peter's did?

The answer is partnership. James and John were partners with Peter in business. So because of partnership, the legal joining of several people into one legal entity, the entire business was blessed when Jesus borrowed the boat. Remember, our working definition of the word *blessed* is "to separate or consecrate." So when Jesus borrowed the boat, the whole business was separated from the government of people to the legal jurisdiction of the government of God. Through a word of knowledge given by Jesus, the Kingdom of God showed Peter where the fish were. Peter, acting on that word, received this huge catch of fish. Now here is the mystery: *James and John simply were the recipients of **Peter's** faith.* This principle of partnership is a powerful spiritual force that we truly need to understand. Paul also taught this same principle in the book of Philippians.

> *I thank my God every time I remember you. In all my prayers for all of you, I always pray with joy because of your partnership in the gospel from the first day until now* (Philippians 1:3-5).

Paul said that he remembers the church in Philippi with joy because of their partnership with him in the Gospel. What exactly was he talking about? We can find the answer toward the close of this letter he wrote to them:

> *Yet it was good of you to share in my troubles. Moreover, as you Philippians know, in the early days of your acquaintance with the gospel, when I set out from Macedonia, not one church shared with me in the matter of giving and receiving, except you only; for even when I was in Thessalonica, you sent me aid again and again when I was in need. Not that I am looking for a gift, but I am looking for what may be credited to your account. I have received full payment and even more; I am amply supplied, now that I have received from Epaphroditus the gifts you sent. They are a fragrant offering, an acceptable sacrifice, pleasing to God. And now my God will meet all your needs according to His glorious riches in Christ Jesus* (Philippians 4:14-19).

We now see why Paul remembered them with joy and what he meant when he said partnership. They were supporting him everywhere he went. In fact, Paul said at one time they were the only ones who were supporting him. He considered them a partner in the Gospel with him. Now let's go back to chapter one and continue from where we left off, and we will see this mystery unfold.

*It is right for me to feel this way about all of you, since I have you in my heart; for whether I am in chains or defending and confirming the gospel, **all of you share in God's grace with me*** (Philippians 1:7 emphasis added).

Paul was saying that because of their partnership with him, they all shared in God's grace with him. We need to notice two very important things about this text. First of all, the church in Philippi now shared in or partook of the same grace that was on Paul's life. Remember, grace is God's ability made available to us. The second thing we need to see is that Paul said the whole church at Philippi shared in his grace, not just the ones who gave the most money. This is because of the members' partnership with each other.

Paul was saying that this church would receive the same exact reward he was receiving because of their partnership with him. (Again, James and John received the same exact boatload of fish as Peter did because of partnership.) Besides the church receiving the same exact reward that Paul got for his labors, the partnership also did something else, and here is the real mystery. The grace that the church now shared, which was on Paul's life, was then able to help supply all their needs according to God's glorious riches in Christ Jesus. What does this mean? It means that Paul was in agreement from his side of the partnership to believe with them for financial increase, just as they were in agreement with his mission to reach people for Christ.

Here is the powerful mystery. James and John received their catch because of Peter's faith. Now the church in Philippi was going to receive what they needed based not only on their faith, but also on Paul's faith. They did their part, they partnered with him, but now his faith would join with theirs to provide a great financial harvest for that church.

Let me translate that into simple, everyday terms. When someone partners with me in ministry, we become partners in the Gospel. Two things happen. First, they receive a reward based on what I do. Or in other words, we will share the same reward for whatever I do in ministry. The second thing it does is it couples my faith with their faith for what *they* need. Let's say that they need $5,000 for a bill coming up. Well, I have to believe God for $100,000 a week to run my ministry, and that number keeps getting bigger. My ability to believe God for $5,000 was developed long ago. To me that seems very easy. So when they partner with me, I am going to agree with them for that $5,000. Now here is the powerful aspect of partnership. That $5,000 can show up because of my faith joined with theirs because of our partnership. Now, they do have to be in agreement with me and release their faith for that $5,000. After all, they are the ones who will have to go and harvest it once God shows them where it is located. They may not have a clue how that money is going to show up. But by partnering with me, their ability to receive that $5,000 has now taken on a new dimension. My faith has legally joined their faith for that $5,000.

Let me share an email that I received that will illustrate this principle.

> Greetings, Pastor Gary.
>
> I wanted to share with you some news that I believe is directly tied to the recent ProVision Conference.
>
> I have been "marinating" on as many teaching CDs from the church, your books, the Now Revolution CDs, as well as my own personal study in the Word regarding finances for months. I did not understand why God kept leading me to study finances when it seemed that there were more important topics to study, like love or forgiveness or faith. However, He kept leading me back to studying biblical financial principles.
>
> I did not realize how much I needed teaching and healing in the area of finances. Yes, I needed to be *healed*

from some incorrect teaching and great pain regarding finances. I had no idea how much confusion and sadness had depleted my ability to fulfill my call and caused much heartsickness.

After all these months, I still have so many questions and so much to learn. However, I have some major dental bills upcoming and decided to reach out in faith to have them met. My doctor estimated that my portion of the bill after insurance would be $13,400. At the ProVision conference, I sowed a seed of $200 dollars. I knew I needed someone to come into agreement with me that had sufficient faith to believe, so I asked Teresa and Ray to pray with me. We agreed that my need would be fully met by October 6th.

Since that time, I kept looking for a way to harvest the money. While I am seeking God to start a business, I knew that I could not prepare the business and collect an income in time to pay the dentist. I kept on in faith moving forward, doing all I knew to do, and continued to speak the Word.

I have worked with the same company for over five years. When I started, there were only eight employees. Now, there are over 80. Three weeks ago, the CEO announced that he was selling the company to Cardinal Health. When the sale was complete last week, he came back to the office to say goodbye. He handed me the attached paper (a check for $13,000).

While all employees received an unexpected bonus check, mine was well over 10 times the amount of theirs. When he handed it to me, he said that he gave me a little extra because he remembered the times that

I stayed until after midnight to ensure that our billing was correct and on time.

I really want to go all the way with God, especially in this area. Now that God has met this need, I am taking another step of faith and using my savings to pay off my only debt—a student loan. I do not want to live life as a hoarder. I give a lot of time and money, but I hoard the rest. It causes me to live a very small life of frustration.

Thank you so very much for your prayers and for teaching me about the freedom and joy God has for us. I consider you and Pastor Drenda to be among the greatest blessings of my lifetime. If I can ever be of service to you, I would gladly do so.

Best Regards,

AG

This young lady had studied these principles, and she was ready to release her faith at my conference. Teresa, the lady she asked to pray for her, was one of the speakers at the conference who shared how these principles had changed the lives of her and her husband.

I first met Teresa while I was doing a conference in North Carolina. She came in with a few other ladies and was just glowing. She shared with me how her family had been just about homeless when she discovered these money mysteries of the Kingdom. By applying these Kingdom principles, within a period of about a year and a half, they now had a business that was prospering. In fact, they paid off their cars, their new house, their business property, and $48,000 in credit card debt, all in less than 20 months!

Both of these stories show how this principle of partnership accelerates the function of faith in the earth realm. This is a powerful principle, but one that many do not understand and consequently do not use to their advantage. What I mean by this is that many people confuse partnership with giving to the poor. The Bible does promise us that if we give to the poor, we are lending to the Lord, and He will repay us (see Prov. 19:17). But giving to the poor, or giving to meet a need, is a different principle than the partnership principle.

When you give to meet someone's need or to help someone, you are partnering with God as I mentioned at the beginning of this chapter. You are not really partnering in the vision of the one you are giving to; you are just reaching out to them in love and helping them. In this type of giving, people are moved by compassion, or sometimes God may actually speak or move on someone to give to a particular need in the life of someone else. But it must be noted that this type of giving is based on the giver's own developed faith.

In the partnership I am now talking about, we actually become partakers of *someone else's faith* by coming into partnership with them. That type of partnership still requires our own faith as well because there is a faith that is released when we walk in partnership. But when we mix our faith together with someone else's vision, and come into agreement in partnership, there is an increase in the grace of God. This is because our faith works together toward a certain result. But here is the key. In order for this partnership to have a positive impact in your life, you want to partner with someone who has faith, knows how faith operates, and has demonstrated good results.

The deception that many people fall prey to is that most of the time, the ministries or people who are successful do not appear to need your money as much as someone else you may know who is struggling. It is a fact that people tend to give to the needy. If a ministry or person is perceived to be doing well, then people will determine that those ministries or people do not need their help, and they will not respond. This, my friend, is not what you should be doing if you really want to propel your finances forward. Now do not misunderstand me; you can give to people and ministries that are struggling all day long, but that giving would be under the "partnering-with-God" category. And God will reward you.

But let's say you were looking for a partner in business. What would you look for? *If you were James and John that day, would you be glad that Peter was your partner?* Or would you want to partner with someone who had fished all night, caught nothing, and *that* ended up being the end of the story? In so many situations, people are sowing to the ministry or person that fished all night and caught nothing. Why? Because it is apparent that they need the help, and people are moved by compassion.

What I am saying is that the ground *where* you sow is just as important as *the seed* you sow, if you are looking for a great return. I get letters all the time from people who are so excited about the Kingdom and want to begin sowing and giving. Then in the same letter they tell me they do not like their church because it is a dead place that is against faith, against the baptism in the Holy Spirit, against prospering, against healing—but they are going to sow their seed there, believing for a return. And in many cases, a return does come because of their own faith. But there is a difference in return when you partner with someone who is on the same page, knows how faith works, agrees with you, and expects the manifestation. This type of ministry is where you want to partner. This is because when you partner, you are participating in their grace—the anointing on their assignment—and that is a powerful combination.

When people partner with Faith Life Now, we promise that we will come into agreement with them and stand with them for the manifestation. Now I am not saying that Faith Life Now is where you should sow—I am just saying that we take it seriously, and so should the ministry with which you partner. God will call all of us to hook up and partner with different people and ministries. Before you sow for increase, just be sure you are sowing in good ground. You can and *should* sow to those in need around you. But when I encourage people to sow for specific financial increase, I always teach them to partner with someone with demonstrated faith and financial integrity. This brings the *overflow* so that they will have the ability to be generous to the poor.

So remember this mystery of partnership—it can be the difference between fishing all night only to catch nothing and *having so much you cannot hold it all!*

||||||||||||||||||||||||||||||||||||||||||||||||||||||||||||||||||||||||||||||||||||||||||||||||||||||||||

Chapter Eight

THE MYSTERY
OF PROFIT

THIS next parable of Jesus has been taught in every Sunday school class in America. It is known as the story of the Good Samaritan. We can easily recall it, and probably if we asked people blindly on the street about it, they could also tell us a version of it. But there is a mystery to this story that no one ever mentions, and no one seems to pick up on, but is a powerful truth concerning money in the earth realm. We have already discussed the fact the Jesus spoke in parables to hide Kingdom truth from the enemy, and there is one here as well. So let's look at this parable and find yet another money mystery of the Kingdom.

> On one occasion, an expert in the law stood up to test Jesus. "Teacher," he said, "what must I do to inherit eternal life?"
>
> "What is written in the law?" Jesus said. "How do you read it?"
>
> He answered, "Love the Lord your God with all your heart and with all your soul and with all your strength and with all of your mind,"; and "Love your neighbor as yourself."

"You have answered correctly," Jesus said. "Do this, and you will live."

But he wanted to justify himself, so he asked Jesus, "And who is my neighbor?"

In reply Jesus said, "A man was going down from Jerusalem to Jericho, when he fell into the hands of robbers. They stripped him of his clothes, beat him, and went away, leaving him half dead. A priest happened to be going down the same road, and when he saw the man, he passed by on the other side. So, too, a Levite, when he came to the place and saw him, passed by on the other side. But a Samaritan, as he traveled, came where the man was; and when he saw him, he took pity on him. He went to him and bandaged his wounds, pouring on oil and wine. Then he put the man on his own donkey, and took him to an inn, and took care of him. The next day, he took out two silver coins and gave them to the innkeeper. 'Look after him,' he said, 'and when I return, I will reimburse you for any extra expense you may have.' Which of these three do you think was the neighbor to the man who fell into the hands of the robber?"

The expert in the law replied, "Well, the one who had mercy on him."

Jesus said, "Go and do likewise" (Luke 10:25-37).

The Pharisees were very, very keyed in on the law; they were very detailed people of the law. They were very much enforcers of the law in their judgmental way. Jesus was obviously confronting a heart issue with them. The parable confronted this man who claimed that he is a righteous man and said to him essentially, "Are you doing this? This is what righteousness includes." But the man answered back to Jesus, "Who's my neighbor?" And the parable was essentially saying, "Well, here's your neighbor. Here's what he looks like. Are you doing this?" The story confronted this Pharisee's self-righteousness.

But like all parables, what you see on the surface is not the entire revelation of the Kingdom, and we want to go a step further and dig deeper into this parable. Now, we know that Jesus was going to illustrate God's heart in His answer to this Pharisee. And in His answer, Jesus was illustrating what God would do if He were there, also implying what this Pharisee should do if he came across this type of situation. So, let's take a different perspective of the parable, and let's envision that this is God reaching out to humanity in this parable. Read it again from that perspective.

> *A man was going down from Jerusalem to Jericho, when*
> *he fell into the hands of robbers. They stripped him of his*
> *clothes, beat him, and went away, leaving him half dead*
> (Luke 10:30).

We can assume that the man beaten and left for dead represents humanity—we have lost our former glory and now find ourselves subject to sin, sickness, poverty, and death through Adam's fall. The Bible says in John 10 that the enemy, satan, comes to steal, kill, and destroy, and so now we find ourselves subject to satan's dominion of darkness. We have been stripped of any dignity and of our former glory as children of God. We lost our authority to rule in life, and we now find ourselves subject to the thief (satan) and fear (represented by the road, as it was a "dangerous road to travel").

In the story, we see Jesus confronting the priest and the religious folks who were self-righteous in their own works and had no real concern for people. Indeed, their only concern was for themselves. Remember, in the last chapter we learned that God loves humanity and is looking for people to partner with Him to reach humanity with His love. Yet, here we see the religious—those who claim to love God—turning away from the very people God loves. Jesus used a Samaritan to make His point because the Jews despised Samaritans and saw themselves as being much more righteous than them. In fact, the Jews despised them so much that they would not even associate with them and would go to any lengths necessary to avoid contact with them for fear that they become unclean.

But the story reveals God's heart for the beaten man and strongly declares the Samaritan as more righteous than the religious clergy. After all, he cared for what God cares for.

> *But a Samaritan, as he traveled, came where the man was, and when he saw him, he took pity on him. He went to him and bandaged his wounds, pouring on oil and wine* (Luke 10:33-34).

The Samaritan not only saw the injured man, but took it upon himself to do something to help him. This is God's heart. He cares for humanity and took it upon Himself to come to us. We did not find God. God sent Jesus after us. He came after you. You were beaten, you were broken, you had nothing to offer, and you were robbed of any worth. God came to you. He sent Jesus to redeem your life.

The story then goes on to say that he went out of his way and bandaged this person, and he poured on oil and wine. Now, in the natural, oil helps heal, and wine is an anesthetic. Both of these, the wine and the oil, have been symbols of a couple of things throughout the entire New Testament. Wine has always represented the blood of Christ. Just as the anesthetic kills the bacteria attacking our bodies, the blood of Christ removes the problem of sin, which holds us hostage to death, both naturally and spiritually. The oil represents the Holy Spirit, who brings us life. The story paints a picture of God taking it upon Himself to meet our need. He came to us and bandaged our wounds, setting us free from the poison of sin, and He poured life back into us by His Spirit.

> *Then he put the man on his own donkey, and took him to*
> *an inn, and took care of him* (Luke 10:34).

The story also says that the Samaritan took it upon himself to carry that man on his own donkey to a place of recovery, which means he gave up his own rights voluntarily and walked. Jesus left His former place of glory to come to earth and die for you and me. Now, that's a great story, the story of salvation.

We can stop right here and celebrate for a while for what God did for us. I think most people can see what we have already brought out from the story—but the story does not end there. A profound mystery about money is about to be revealed in this story.

> *The next day, he took out two silver coins and gave them*
> *to the innkeeper. "Look after him," he said, "and when I*
> *return, I will reimburse you for any extra expense you may*
> *have"* (Luke 10:35).

Why did God talk about money in this story? He could have left the story after He made His point to the Pharisees—but He didn't because there's *much* more here.

We can see that after the Samaritan took this man to the inn, it says that the next day he took out two silver coins and gave them to the innkeeper. "*Look after him,' he said, 'and when I return, I will reimburse you for any extra expense you may have.'*" Again, why does He make a point of mentioning money? What is God saying? We have already concluded that this Samaritan, who in this story represents the heart of God for humanity, takes upon himself the burden and cost to help this beaten stranger left for dead along the roadside. We see the Samaritan taking this man to an inn because the man is too wounded to travel and needs time to rest and recover. The Samaritan prepays the inn keeper with two silver coins and then says something so profound I had to stop and reread it several times to be sure I had it right.

"Look after him," he said, "and when I return, I will reimburse you for any extra expense you may have."

Whoa! Rewind! Let's look at what he said in slow motion, *"When I return, I will reimburse you for **any extra expense you may have**."* Remember, the Samaritan in this story represents God, and he is telling the innkeeper that all of the expense needed to take care of this man—whatever it takes, whatever it costs—will be covered. That is the first mystery revealed. **God will pay the bills for you to act on His behalf to help people.**

Now here is the second part of the mystery: *you are the innkeeper.* The Church is the inn that takes the broken and dying after the blood and Spirit have been applied, and the Church allows the broken to heal and become whole. The Church is not a building—you are the Church. You are the doctor of humanity. You are the one Jesus empowered to go and touch people, the one who brings the oil and the wine. The Church is the institution of God in the earth realm to reach out to people and to bring them to healing and wholeness. And here is God's promise to the innkeeper: *"**Whatever it costs!**"* This gives you a perspective of what God considers important to Him and how small He views the value of money compared to the value of a person.

I just finished building an $8 million dollar facility here in Ohio called the Now Center, where my church meets. Do you know what God says about it? "Whatever it costs." You know, He's not concerned about $8 million. He doesn't look at it and go, "That's just too much money, man. You've gotta be kidding." He would say, "Whatever it costs." God has a whatever-it-costs perspective on money, because He's not after money. He's after people. Money is not His issue. His issue is people, and He will go to all extremes and all costs to reach just one person. He left that innkeeper with *a totally blank check!*

Someone may say, "Well, I believe that God is talking about when Jesus comes back in this story, and that is when we will get our reward." The Bible *does* say that Jesus will come back, and He will have our reward with Him (see Eph. 6:8), but I don't believe that is the total picture of what God is saying here. He is talking about taking care of people here and *now* in the earth realm. Once the Lord returns, it's too late to reach people. The innkeeper has to be paid *now* to reach the lost and broken. In this particular story, the Samaritan traveled this road as a businessman, probably many times a month or year. That is evident from the fact that the innkeeper took the Samaritan at his word and extended him credit toward the bill associated with taking care of this man.

Remember, you are the innkeeper, and here is what God is saying to you: "I'll make sure that you are amply supplied to carry out the assignment I have given you. Take care of people." And again, God says, *"Whatever it costs!"* If that is not enough good news, there is an even deeper and greater mystery here.

The Church of today has the religious thing down. "Oh, I know I'm supposed to help the guy who's been beaten. I know that I am supposed to help feed the poor. I know I should help in the nursery at church. I know I'm supposed to do this for God! I'm supposed to give it all away for God. I'm just supposed to lay it all down for God. It's all about God!" That is a religious martyrdom mindset! But that's how we have all been trained. Religion is a hard taskmaster, right? So even if we hear that God will pay all the bills for us to go out and serve Him, we somehow still feel like that is a duty. We miss the whole point!

The innkeeper did not hear the Samaritans request to take care of the stranger as if it were a duty. He didn't hear it as, "You have to take care of him. Look, he's been beaten up. I mean, come on, buddy! Don't you have compassion? Look at the guy! You have to help us out and do it for free!" Is that what he said to the innkeeper? He did not. So how did the innkeeper hear the request? Let me tell you how he heard the words of that Samaritan: *He heard profit!*

He didn't hear anything about duty. He didn't hear anything about religion. He didn't hear anything except that he was going to be *paid* for all the days he would take care of this guy. The Samaritan was speaking this hotel owner's language—*profit!*

Now that begins to change things, doesn't it? It's strange; the Church doesn't have a profit mentality. They have a duty mentality, a poverty mentality. That innkeeper heard the word *profit*. You can get really spiritual and say, "Well, you know, you're supposed to do this and supposed to do that." But listen, God is about profit, all kinds of profit. He wants His Kingdom to expand. *He* wants to profit. And He wants *you* to have a profit mindset. God wants you to understand that if you hook up with Him, He's going to pay you. He's going to pay you full wages. He's going to take good care of you. There's profit in serving God. This is the part that we miss in the story of the Good Samaritan, but it's one of the greatest money mysteries of the Kingdom!

Let me give yet another story in the Bible that we have heard our entire lives, and yet this lesson of profit is never told along with it. But without it, the story would probably never have happened. Let's revisit the story of David and Goliath.

> *When the Israelites saw the man [Goliath], they all ran from him in great fear. Now, the Israelites had been saying, "Do you see how this man keeps coming out? He keeps coming out to defy Israel. The king will give great wealth to the man who kills him. He will also give him his daughter in marriage and will exempt his father's family from taxes in Israel"* (1 Samuel 17:24-25).

When David got to the battle line, do you know the first thing David asked the men standing around him? It wasn't, "What are we going to do?" or "Listen guys, God has done so much for us, it is our duty to die defending Israel." No! Instead, his first question was, *"What will be done for the man who takes care of this Philistine...?"* (1 Sam. 17:26).

What was David thinking about? Profit! David was profit-minded. He asked several people around him, continually, "What will be done for this man who takes care of the problem?" Profit. In fact, the Bible records that he asked three times about the reward, just to be sure he had it right. For some reason, the Church feels guilty and ashamed to talk about profit. But I am telling you that is how God thinks. And when you hook up with Him, He is going to make sure that you will profit with Him as you work in the Kingdom together.

Profit: another hidden mystery of the Kingdom!

||||||||||||||||||||||||||||||||||||||||||||||||||||||||||||||||||||||||||||||||||||||||||||||||||||||||||

Chapter Nine

THE MYSTERY
OF THE ASSIGNMENT

Who serves as a soldier at his own expense? Who plants a vineyard and does not eat of its grapes? Who tends a flock and does not drink of the milk? (1 Corinthians 9:7)

LET'S add this to our list of things we need to know about God: *He funds His assignments.* I know, I know, you already know that right? Well, if you look at most Christians' lives, you would think otherwise. It seems most Christians are waiting for God to send them a check in the mail and have no real idea *how* God funds His Kingdom in the earth realm. Again, I call it the "mailbox mentality." It is incredible that Christians *wait around* hoping God is just going to have someone hand them a check for a million dollars. You may ask me why I would think that way. It's because if you ask most Christians where the money is going to show up, they can't answer you. They can't name a business that they believe God will bless or an idea that they are working to launch. Usually, if a believer has a need for money, and you ask them where they are going to get it, they simply say God is going to bring it to them. And...?

Well, I do believe that God will provide all we need, but the question is, *how* is He going to do that? *Where* is it going to show up?

Let's face it—the world worships money. They are not going to give you any of their money unless you can solve a problem or handle responsibility for them. So when people come to me and ask me how to make more money, I tell them to solve a bigger problem or take on more responsibility. And that is exactly what this next parable shows us. This story in Matthew 25 reveals yet another money mystery of the Master.

> *Again, [the kingdom is]...like a man going on a journey, who called his servants and entrusted his property to them. To one, he gave five talents of money, to another two talents, and to another, one talent,* **each according to his ability***...* (Matthew 25:14-15).

Just a quick note before we continue. When the Bible says *talents* here, Matthew is not talking about singing or painting, as most people think of *talents*. Matthew is talking about money. The *talent* is a monetary unit used in ancient times. In the Greek unit of weight it was about 60 pounds.

> *The man who had received the five talents went at once and put his money to work and gained five more. So also, the one with the two talents gained two more, but the man who had received the one talent went off, dug a hole in the ground and hid his master's money. After a long time the master of those servants returned and settled accounts with them. The man who had received the five talents brought the other five. 'Master,' he said, 'you entrusted me with five talents. See, I have gained five more'* (Matthew 25:16-20).

Let's talk about this for a minute. Let's assume that you would like to have a lot of money (talents). How would you go about obtaining the money you desired? How many of you have looked in your backyard and found it doesn't grow on trees? Rather, money is a function of a marketplace transaction of business and commerce. There are no dollar bills in Heaven, so if you want money you can spend here, you have to operate with wisdom in this realm to either capture or create wealth.

In this particular parable, the master (who is God) gave an assignment based on the person's ability. One servant received five talents, one received two, and one received one. The first thing I want to focus on is the relationship between the number of talents, or how much money each servant received, and their ability. To help me explain this, let me ask you a question. What would happen if the guy who had five talents really desired ten instead of five? Have you ever done that before? Maybe, after seeing a really sharp sports car go by, you said to yourself, "Wow, I wish I had a car like that." You may even have thought that the guy in the sports car was just lucky. But you need to remember that luck probably had very little to do with it. Because money does not grow on trees, you can assume there must be something the driver knows about money in the earth realm that allowed him to buy a car like that. (I am assuming, of course, that he is not up to his eyeballs in debt and actually owns the car outright.)

The problem is most people are not interested in learning the process that got the driver that car. He had to posture himself to acquire the means to buy such a car. Instead, people are just interested in the fancy sports car. This is where people tend to focus on the wrong thing. Instead of the car, we should be focused on what the driver knows. Apparently, he knows something we don't know, something that he learned. It's something we could also learn if we would stop wishing and start paying attention.

So, let's assume that guy with five talents wished he had ten or the guy with one talent wished he had two, or ten, or fifty, or a million. The problem is the guy who had the five talents was given that much based on *his ability.* That means he's a five-talent guy, right? He's a five-talent guy because that's all the responsibility he could handle. So, even if he desires to have more than five talents, how many can he realistically have? Only five, because that is the level of responsibility he can handle. Unless something changes (his level of ability and responsibility), he will be destined to manage five talents for the rest of his life. Even if by chance he stumbles onto a million talents, he will end up losing them because he only has the ability to manage five talents. So here is my question: **how much can God trust you with?**

The last time I checked, the world pays people money to handle responsibility or to solve problems or to fix things. So if you are a five-talent person, you are going to live at a five-talent income until you die—*unless you change.* You may ask me what you need to change, and I would say that there are usually a couple things most people need to change. At the top of the list, I would put, "How much weight can you carry, and how much responsibility can you handle?" If you want more pay, you have to handle more weight.

I remember sitting in a sales training seminar when I was younger, and this statement really stuck with me, "Gary, you can judge someone's success by how fast they deal with and get rid of negatives." Every sales rep I ever trained wants to focus on the details, the little minor details. They have no clients. They have no activity. But they want to just focus on little details, just in case they *do* get a client. When they finally do get a client, they fuss and worry about that one client, worrying if they can close the deal. Then they stop doing anything and focus on that one client until they get a check in their hand from that case. But a seasoned sales manager knows that the new rep is focusing on the wrong thing. He knows that the new sales rep needs to focus on the big picture, which is having more clients than he can even schedule. The sales manager knows that we can always figure the details out later, but first he must have a reason to know those details. How fast can you deal with the negatives? That's what you are paid to do. Anyone could make a sale if there was a long line out their door of people wanting to buy what they sell. Sales people are not paid to write up the sale—they are paid to go through the *no's* to find the *yes*. They are paid to find the people who want to buy.

Now, we are not just talking about sales here. Having a problem that you need to solve is a negative that needs an answer. It's also a negative to be asked to do something you have no experience in, with no clue where to start. People do not like dealing with the negatives, facing uncomfortable situations, stretching themselves outside their comfort zone, and facing their weaknesses. But they must if they want to grow.

Several years ago, my church had grown to about 300 people, and the mom-and-pop model of pastoring my church was starting to kill me. I could not keep up with everyone, and the demands on me personally brought me to a breaking point. So I began to hire more staff to help me. However, I knew nothing about how to hire church employees or how to manage them. I was a sales trainer and sales people are self-starters. They either make it or not based on their own ability. But having an employee was a completely different issue. They had to be paid with or without results. I thought just having more staff would be my answer. But do you know what? It got worse. The more employees I hired, the worse it became. I had less time than before. I had to attend more meetings, do more training, do more crisis solving then I had done when it was just me. Finally, I could not take it anymore. I was finished. I just felt that I was not cut out to be a pastor, and I wanted to resign.

At the time, my church owned 23 acres of land that was paid for and would be the site of our new complex someday. But during the previous three years I had not walked on that land one time. I just could not handle the chaos that I was already experiencing, and I did not want to magnify it by making it bigger. I was in survival mode and sinking. But Drenda had heard of a man who helped pastors learn how to lead, and we attended one of his seminars. I was deeply moved by what I heard; it all made sense. I realized I just needed some training on how to do my job. I was not a failure. I just needed training. That simple fact freed me from the constant discouragement I faced each day. It gave me hope. After the seminar, I was the first in line to talk to the speaker, and I asked him if he did any one-on-one training and if he would please help me learn how to do my job. He said yes, and I set up my training right there on the spot. Dean Radtke is his name, and he has a passion to help pastors understand what corporate America has known for a long time concerning leadership training.

One of the first things that Dean said to me was, "It will get worse, but you've got to get better." I thought, *Well, I am not sure I can handle any more!* But Dean continued and said, "Yes, it *will* get worse, but you *can* get better." When he first told me that, I wanted to puke. I said, "You've got to be kidding me. I can't bear anything worse. I'm having a struggle keeping up right now! How do you do that?" Dean looked right at me and said, "You've got to learn. You've got to change. You have to adapt and adjust. Your ability to handle responsibility has to change!" I learned very quickly the things I was doing wrong and the things I needed to learn how to do.

I had to let go of five of my staff members because I had hired the wrong people for the job. Many were my personal friends who had been there since the beginning of the church. There was great pain in the decisions I had to make, but I had to make them. But that's when my life changed. By saying *yes* to my assignment *and* learning how to do it, the church grew from 300 members to 1,500 members in six years. During those six years, we built the Now Center campus, started our Life Leadership College, launched our Faith Life Now international television broadcasts (*Fixing the Money Thing* and *Drenda*), created and hosted multiple conferences around the globe, published books, and started our marketplace ministry school, Provision Institute. During this same time my companies grew and prospered. And you know what? My wife now has one of those fancy sports cars, which I paid cash for. So if you see me driving down the street in her car and you are tempted to think, "Wow, he is just lucky," I would point you to this parable, and it would give you the process you need to access *your* future.

So let's review for a bit. We have discussed the fact that we need to change; we need to grow in our ability to handle more weight. It is interesting that when I talk to business people about their businesses and tell them that God wants to help them, they usually interpret what I am saying as "God is going to bring all the customers I can handle to my business." They think I mean that God will *make* their business successful. *Wrong!* I try to tell them that their current business model is functioning and producing profit based on its current structure and efficiency. There is only one way for that business to become more profitable—the business must change! This same need for change is true for us as individuals and leaders, as well. When we feel overwhelmed or frustrated, we are maxed out and must recognize that if we are going to handle more responsibility, we must change the processes and methods we currently use.

But how do we change? That process is revealed in this parable, as well. The master understood how to use it effectively to train His servants to prosper on His behalf, and He will work with us through that same process if we will let Him.

So let's look back at the story. Remember the guy who was given the five talents and ended up with ten talents? The master gave him the five talents based on his current ability. *But* here is the mystery. Did the master give him a five-talent assignment? We can falsely believe that is what happened, but the text does not say how big the assignment was, does it? No, it does not say that the master gave him a five-talent assignment; it just says that the master gave the assignments out based on each servant's current ability. We know the final result: the guy brought home ten talents, not five. In my thinking, it takes a ten-talent assignment to produce ten talents. I believe the only reason that guy got paid ten talents was because he tackled a ten-talent assignment. He put that money to work in a project or an assignment that had a ten-talent potential return.

He was a five-talent guy, but the master gave him an assignment that was bigger than what he was currently managing. The master knew that the servant had the capacity to stretch and grow to the next level. He knew that the only way for that servant to grow and change was *not* to just get by with doing the same thing he did yesterday, over and over and over again. It would require him engaging in bigger and bigger projects as he matured. In so doing, he made himself more valuable as a manager to the master and to himself. When he stood there before the master after the assignment was completed, he had grown. He was no longer a five-talent guy; he was now a ten-talent guy. He had changed.

There was something else about this servant that I want to point out. If you face a responsibility that you feel you are not currently able to handle, especially when handling someone else's money, you will agree that fear can get involved. The natural inclination would be to take the easy way out and play it safe. I would like to point out that this servant went *immediately* and put the money to work. He did not procrastinate, even though he had to cast down the feelings of fear he faced concerning this new assignment. This obviously was not the first time he had been given an assignment from his master.

We can assume that he had learned from previous experience that if his master thought he could do it, then—even though there was fear involved—he could jump into it with both feet. He trusted that the master would not give him an assignment beyond **his current ability to stretch and grow.** He had found that the master was good and could be trusted. The servant had learned from past assignments that the pressure, frustration, and hard work would be to his advantage, bringing promotion, profit, and reward. The master knew how to use the one element that was essential to the servant's promotion and future—*pressure!*

Pressure is the only thing that stretches things.

Learn this principle; you can read all about managing the processes that may be required for an assignment, but it's only by engaging the actual process and dealing with the pressure that you actually change. I compare the process to marriage. You can read countless books on marriage and learn some things, but only being married and having to lay your life down on a daily basis will mold you into a great spouse.

So the next time you cry out to God for help, plead for greater income, and say, "God, I need some help; I need more money!" There is only one thing He can do for you, and that is to give you a big assignment. He will bring opportunities that look bigger than you along your path, and you have to embrace those things and jump in there. Remember, money doesn't grow on trees. But people will pay out money all day long to someone who solves problems for them. That is where you will shine because the Holy Spirit lives in you and will help you with the solutions to the problems. What He leads you to capture, He will provide the battle plan to obtain. Will there be stress? Yes! Can there be fearful moments? For sure! Will there be frustrations? I hope so. Frustration is the breeding ground of change, as Dr. Radtke says.

The people in my church know I have a phrase that I like to use a lot. *If you are not doing the hardest thing you have ever done, then you are not growing.*

Don't try to have all the answers before you take on an assignment. It is impossible to see all the details or the full dynamic of any situation until you wade in there and figure it out. Just know that the pressure is working in your best interest. You are changing!

I teach my family, my church, and myself to just say *yes* to God's direction and assignments. If you don't have a clue how to do it, just say, "Yes, I can do that," kind of like my friend who committed to bake cheesecake for that healthfood chain, and he didn't even have a bakery!

But he got the contract. And God provided the way after he said *yes.* Someone may ask, "Well then, how are you going to do it? You have never done that before?" And my answer would go something like this—and get ready, this is a very spiritual answer that you will not want to miss—I'd say, "I don't know, I haven't gotten that far yet."

Seriously, one thing I have learned is that you have to engage the opportunities that come along your path. God will make sure they come, but you have to engage those opportunities. Here is the cool thing. You are not alone, because He's your wisdom. He will help you with people. He will bring consultants. He will surround you with people who can help you stretch. So go ahead and stretch.

Sadly, the Church is full of disillusioned people who are weak and think that anytime they come up against pressure they have missed God. The one phrase that I heard Art Williams say over and over again as I worked with him was, "No one wants to follow a dull, disillusioned, frustrated crybaby." People who are always complaining about God, complaining about church, complaining about life, complaining about their problems, hoping someone will give them some money, will never attract anything good.

No! God leads us into pressure to stretch us and to give us a platform for victory and promotion. It's time we understood how this thing works. We need to understand the process. We're not babies anymore. We're not immature. We're to be mature and know how this thing operates. God is going to ask us to do some big stuff. He is going to give us big dreams, and we have to understand that those dreams will require us to stretch. We're going to have to grow to get it done. I have lived most of my life scared. I keep saying *yes* to God and doing things that scare me spitless. Listen, you can be afraid and move forward. As Joyce Meyer says, "Do it afraid!" Even though I feel afraid, I press forward trusting God will back me up. That is how we have done everything we have done.

This spring we launched a women's television program called *Drenda*. Obviously, it is a show hosted by my wife Drenda that is geared to address the issues that face women and the families of America. In case you did not know it, our country is falling apart due to immorality and unrighteousness. My wife has raised five babies successfully, helped me start three companies, started our church, launched a television program, managed the building of the Now Center, and been the catalyst for everything else we have done. She is well qualified to confront the filth streaming from the mainstream media.

At first, we thought we would just launch an Internet television channel, but all of a sudden ABC Family heard about the show and wanted a pilot. After seeing the pilot, they said they wanted the program. Only one little snag—it would cost us about $40,000 a month on top of our $65,000 television budget. What would you say at that moment? I have been through this process many times now. I am well aware of the Matthew 25 principle. So we said *yes*. "You mean, Gary, you guys said yes to ABC Family without knowing where the budget was going to come from? Isn't that a little presumptuous?" Well, it could have been if our heart was wrong and if this was our first time out. But we have been here many times before, and we wanted to seize this territory for God. He spoke to my wife to do this. We knew it would take faith and courage, but we felt that God was leading us to take that territory. So after we said *yes*, we told our church what we felt God had for us to do, and they were so excited that in one weekend they gave $240,000 toward the project! But I would not be totally honest if I did not tell you that I had to face some fear in making that decision.

One night, the enemy woke me up with fear and began to torment me with all the things that could go wrong and with questions like, "Why do you want to do that anyway?" But I have heard that voice every time I have stepped into a new assignment. And you will too. The key is to know how to handle fear and cast down those imaginations the enemy uses to discourage you from taking on any new assignments.

So let me say that the prevailing concept "if it's God, it's going to be easy" is totally false. Just remember that God is right there with you in that battle, and when you win, He gets the glory and you get the promotion. That's a great deal.

Pressure will change your life, but if you yield to fear, it can cripple you. It can make you negative, disillusioned, despondent, withdrawn, and insecure, *or* you can embrace pressure as an opportunity. How you approach it is really the key.

A great example of this was embodied in a salesman I once hired for my Tulsa office. His name was Jim and he was from New York. Fast-talking Jim was always going to do great things. In fact, if you heard him talk, he was going to take on the world. "Man, we're going to do it big, Gary! Do it big, Gary! We're going to do it big!"

He was always pumped up, always bouncing off the walls. But every time I got the monthly production charts, there would be little or no production listed for Jim. He was starving and barely making it. I'll never forget the time I saw his silver Honda Civic coming down the freeway toward our office. My office was on the fifth floor and it was all windows, and I could see the freeway as it ran beside my office. So one morning I spotted this silver Honda Civic going really slow, being passed right and left. I could tell it was Jim's car. Being from New York, Jim always drove very fast, but this particular morning he was being passed in every lane. I thought, "That can't be Jim." But the more I watched, I was convinced it was Jim. I thought, *What is wrong with Jim's car?*

As Jim pulled into the parking lot, I ran down to meet him. "Jim, what's wrong with your car? You OK? You need help? I've never seen you drive that slow before."

"Oh, no," he says. "Come here, I'll show you something."

He had a big smirk on his face. "My license tag expired," he admitted. "See, I've got this big maple leaf stuck inside the license tag holder in the back to cover the expired sticker. I had to drive slow enough so that the leaf wouldn't blow out of there. To avoid suspension, I had to drive the speed limit."

Folks, that was the story of Jim's life. I'm serious. Do you know people like that? I mean, if it wasn't the license tags, it was something else the next week—constantly some disaster, some emotional problem, some financial chaos. It was always survival at Jim's house. But if you ever heard him talk, it was always, "Wow, we're gonna tear it up, I mean tear it up!" Jim *would have* torn it up if he had ever made the phone calls that were needed to really tear it up.

Eventually the Lord told me to move from Tulsa back to Ohio, and I was going to shut my office down in Tulsa. Jim was going to transfer to another local office. One day Jim came in and pulled the door shut without inviting himself. He just pulled the door shut and sat down. "Gary," he said, "I want to let you know something. I've paid an awesome price here for two years with you. I've paid an awesome price."

I cut him off. I knew what was going to happen. I knew behind that was going to come the complaining and the whining and "You didn't train me enough," and all that garbage. I said, "Yeah, Jim, you're right. You know, you did pay an awesome price here. But you know what, Jim? You paid the wrong price. You paid the price of failure." There is a price to pay either for success or failure. And I said, "Jim, you have paid the wrong price. You could have been on the phone, Jim. You could have been talking to clients. You didn't have to drag your wife through this mess. You could have done what you said you were going to do. But you didn't do it, Jim! You just sat there and played survival all those years! Yeah, you paid a price, all right. You learned how to sell things, but not what we were selling. You sold everything you owned at the pawn shops." I said, "Jim, I pray that you understand that unless you change, life is not going to change for you."

I got a call from Jim several years later, after our company moved to Columbus and became the number one office out of 5,000 offices for one of our vendors. Somehow, Jim heard of what we were doing. He called me and said, "Wow, I heard you guys are doing great and that you are number one. That's just great!"

Then he began to talk to me about the ministry he was starting. Interesting how people that fail financially always think they should go into ministry, isn't it? My wife is bold and sometimes tells people who want to go into ministry, "I agree you are called, but you need to learn how to make some money first. Learn how to pay your bills and walk in financial integrity first." That is usually not the answer they really want to hear at that moment.

So anyway, Jim starts to talk about this ministry. "Oh, Gary," he said. "The organization that ordained me has two different membership levels," he said. "One is $75 for an organization, and the other is $10 per person." He then says, "What do you suggest Gary? I do have an organization, but I thought I would just sign up as an individual since it is only ten bucks."

I thought, *Jim, you are still missing the whole deal. You haven't changed in ten years. You are penny-pinching your life and still concerned about sixty bucks? Ten years down the road you are still thinking about sixty bucks?* I felt sorry for Jim as we ended the call. It was nice of him to call, but it was sad to see him still a slave, still in survival mode. So let me ask you a question. Are you just surviving the pressure, or do you have a plan out? Listen, endurance is not the key to success. Let me say it again. Endurance is not the key to success. If you get up in the morning and you don't have a plan, you are not going anywhere.

Some of us in Christianity, on the other hand, are living in little teeny two-talent jobs believing we will have a miraculous million-dollar payout someday. Ain't gonna happen! Just go ahead and chalk it up. Not gonna happen. Remember this money mystery of the Master—God will lead you to an assignment where you will need to stretch and grow. He does it for your good and the good of the Kingdom.

But there is yet still another side to this story we need to talk about, and it's where we will find the real money mystery. It's the story of the servant who did nothing with the one talent that the master gave him. Instead of doing anything with the talent, he just hid it in the ground. At first that sounds like a noble thing, but we will find out that it was not. If you buy into the same mentality, you will also miss what God has for you. Listen to what the servant said to the master regarding his poor performance.

> *Then the man who had received the one talent came. "Master," he said, "I knew that you are a hard man, harvesting where you have not sown and gathering where you have not scattered seed. So I was afraid and went out and hid your talent in the ground. See, here is what belongs to you"* (Matthew 25:24-25 NKJV).

This servant had a wrong perspective of God, accusing Him of being unfair and a hard taskmaster. This is the attitude toward God that religion teaches us—serve, serve, serve. We see people who are supposed to be committed to God being taught that if they really want to serve God they should forsake marriage or live as a pauper in horrible circumstances, all in the name of God. This servant thought there was nothing in it for him, and he did not see the talent as a place of promotion, but as a duty and drudgery. But he was deceived. He did the least he could with the talent, and because of his fear, he hid it so he would not lose it. But he missed the whole point and did not truly know the heart of the master. The master corrects this wicked and lazy service, and in the process, he reveals another powerful money mystery of the Master.

*His master replied, "You wicked and lazy servant! So you knew that I harvest where I have I have not sown and gather where I have not scattered seed? Well, then, you should have put my money on deposit with the bankers, so that when I returned, I would have received it back with interest. Take the talent from him and **give it to the one who has the ten talents. For anyone who has will be given more, and he will have an abundance. Whoever does not have, even what he has will be taken from him.** And throw that worthless servant outside, into the darkness, where there will be weeping and gnashing of teeth"* (Matthew 25:26-30).

Do you see it? The master took the talent that the servant had hidden and gave it to whom? Not the one with four, but the one with ten. Why? Because God knew that this servant would do something with it, something that would increase his profits and his kingdom. Here's the mystery: **God is profit motivated, and He will give more to those who can handle more, to those who have that same mindset!** God's profit is people, and that's what He gave everything to gain back through the cross. He wants increase in His Kingdom, and if He can find someone who has His heart and will use the resources at hand to get that done, then God will bless that person with more. Again, He gives seed to the *sower.*

So in this chapter we learned that God is good; He is not a hard taskmaster. He will lead us into assignments where we will stretch and grow. We take on those hard assignments because we know that God is good and that He is a rewarder of those who carry out His mandates. We know that He will only lead us to the assignments He believes we can handle—with His help. If we continually say *yes* to God, we will be blessed because God is interested in increase!

I know firsthand how God blesses His kids who say *yes*. Man, God blesses me! He just blesses me. He is good! Ask my kids why they are serving God today. My kids are not running away from God, like so many pastors' kids do, because they know He is good. They have seen too much. They are blessed. Most of them are now in their 20s, and God has brought them amazing mates, their cars are paid for, and some of them even have houses that are almost paid off, as well. They have seen God's goodness over and over again. They have traveled the world, seen many things they have wanted to see, and are blessed with good stuff.

In fact, as I write this chapter, my whole family and their spouses are on a cruise ship halfway across the Atlantic on our way to Spain and Italy for three weeks—and it is all paid for. You may say that my kids are just spoiled, but no, I disagree. You see, my kids are God's favorites. Now, before you get offended, let me say that God has plenty of room for favorites. His favorites are the kids who will do anything for Him, who will take on an impossible task and bring glory and profit to the master.

Often my kids will work 50 plus hours a week in the ministry saying *yes* to God's mandates. They have always been that way. They love God so much! We would always have to tell them that they had to come home from church as they grew up, but they always begged to go and serve. You may ask why they were like that. Two reasons. One, they saw their mom and dad operate that way. Two, they saw the goodness of God. They have tasted the Lord's goodness, and they have seen He is extremely good. They found and understood the message of this parable, that there is reward in serving the King of kings. When given an assignment, they go immediately to work to get it done, not with a wicked heart to just do as little as they can, but they do it with their whole hearts as unto the Lord. And they prosper!

And if you have the same heart and take on the assignments that are bigger than you, you will increase and prosper in life, as well. Be one of God's favorites!

Chapter Ten

THE MYSTERY
OF A TRUST

I am going to give you another money mystery of the Master that will be a major key to your future. Very simply, you must pass the money test! Before God will show you the mystery of your destiny and show you great wealth, you will have to pass the money test.

Mike and Stacy came to my church after hearing me on the radio talking about money. They were desperate, about to be evicted out of their apartment, and surviving by scouring the trash piles along the road for useful things they could scavenge. They had both been in the bar business when they first met. Mike was the bar bouncer and Stacy was the barmaid. They had just given their hearts to Christ and really did not know much about the Kingdom, except they were hungry for change. When they called our office, I sent one of my experienced managers over to their apartment. There he told them about being baptized in the Holy Spirit and told them about my church, which they began to attend. The church was small back then, but they were excited. As they heard about the Kingdom, they knew that they needed to work with

God toward their future. They began to hear how important giving was and knew they needed to sow.

Mike was the usher at the front door of the church, and one day he saw a family come to church all crammed in a really little car. Mike did not have any money, but he did have an older white van that he was planning to sell. But now, instead of selling the van, he decided to give that van to the family that was all crammed up in that little car. Mike sowed that van believing that God would help them get a better car for themselves. It was just a few weeks later when they saw a sign at the gym where both Stacy and Mike worked out that described a contest in which the person who lost the most inches over a set period of time would win a new car. They both thought that they could do that. They were so serious that they even paid a personal trainer $500 a month to help them. Mike said that was serious money at the time.

As I pulled into the church one Sunday morning, I saw Mike leaning up against a brand-new, maroon, limited edition Corvette. He had parked it at the front door and was telling anyone who would listen about what they had done and how they had won the contest. Stacy had won the contest! They sold the special car the next day to pay off some debts. You see Mike and Stacy were passing the money test.

That first faith victory encouraged them greatly toward the Kingdom of God, so they launched out and started a business. For the first time, they began to actually have a little extra money. Slowly their lives were changing. I saw their giving to the church begin to improve. The checks began to grow in size from tens to hundreds and then to the occasional thousand dollar check. One day, Mike walked up to me and handed me a check for $5,000 to pay for a conference that I was about to do in Albania. Mike loved the Kingdom of God, and he would tell anyone who would listen about how Jesus had changed his life.

By this time, God had spoken to us to launch a television ministry. We had no money, but we felt confident that God had spoken to us about it and would provide for it. In our first year of television, a network called us and offered us a slot on their network. At the time, we did not have the money to even consider it. But we knew we should pray about it, and if we felt God said to go for it, we would sign the contract, money or not. On that Friday, my family joined to pray about this venture. We had to let the network know by Monday if we wanted to take the offer. That Sunday morning at church, Mike walked up to me with tears in his eyes and said that the Lord had spoken to him and he wanted to give $10,000 a month toward television. He knew nothing of the pending contract. I was shocked. I did not know Mike was even able to make that kind of money, but I thanked him and agreed with him for the money. We said *yes* to the network, and Mike and Stacy were faithful to give that $10,000 a month for one year as they promised.

Mike said that in a few of those months they barely made $10,000, and it was with real faith and commitment that they sowed that $10,000. But their income continued to grow. After the year was up, their business went through a period of major change. In that season of transition, they started a new business, and it began to prosper in a big way. That new business is now bringing in hundreds of thousands of dollars a year to Mike's family. It is now positioned to produce millions as it expands across the county. You see, Mike had to pass the money test before God could really bless him. Mike's heart was tested. If Mike could be trusted with a few thousand dollars and keep his heart and his money available to the Kingdom, then he could be trusted with millions later on. Jesus talked about this very thing in the following parable.

> *Jesus told His disciples, "There was a rich man, whose manager was accused of wasting his possessions. So, he called him in and asked him, 'What is this I hear about you? Give an account of your management, because you cannot be manager any longer.' The manager said to himself, 'What shall I do now? My master is taking away my job. I'm not strong enough to dig, and I'm ashamed to beg.*

I know what I'll do, so that when I lose my job here, people will welcome me into their houses.'

So, he called each one of his master's debtors. He asked the first, 'How much do you owe my master?' 'Eight hundred gallons of olive oil,' he replied. The manager said, 'Take your bill, sit down quickly, and make it four hundred.' Then he asked the second, 'And how much do you owe?' 'A thousand bushels of wheat,' he replied. He told him, 'Take your bill and make it eight hundred.'

The master commended the dishonest manager, because he had acted shrewdly. The people of this world are shrewder in dealing with their own kind than are the people of the light. I tell you, use worldly wealth to gain friends for yourselves, so that when it is gone, you'll be welcomed into eternal dwellings.

Whoever can be trusted with very little can also be trusted with much, and whoever is dishonest with very little will also be dishonest with much. So, if you've not been trustworthy in handling worldly wealth, who will trust you with true riches? And if you've not been trustworthy with someone else's property, who will give you property of your own? No servant can serve two masters. Either he will hate the one and love the other, or he will be devoted to the one and despise the other. You cannot serve both God and money" (Luke 16:1-13).

I have heard so many people say that *when God prospers them* they will give a large amount to the Kingdom of God, but what they do not know is that they just failed the money test. The test is not relative to how much you have, but how you handle what you do have. In this story, Jesus was saying that this dishonest manager was misusing the master's wealth. He did not really value the master's money and was not diligent to manage it for the master's benefit. But when he was about to lose his job, he demonstrated his ability to be shrewd toward his own interest. Although he had the ability to be shrewd toward his own interests, he was unwilling to do so toward the master's interests. In other words, this manager was not aggressively managing the master's money to gain profit.

This story is profound. Can you be trusted with worldly wealth? Jesus tells us here to spend our worldly wealth on God's passion—people—and not ourselves. If we pass that money test, then Jesus says we can be trusted with true riches. I believe the true riches He speaks of represent more than just money, as it speaks of a person's whole life. For example, the peace that people find in discovering their God-breathed passion and destiny, as compared to living just for money and temporary things, is invaluable. But besides the peace and contentment that serving God provides, I also believe these "true riches" include the wealth that God Himself wants to put in our hands to be used on behalf of people and His purposes in the earth.

In contrast, people who have not passed the money test will view the money that comes into their hands as theirs to use as they desire and to consume with their own lusts. But Jesus tells us here that if we would be proven trustworthy with worldly wealth, we could be trusted with much more.

If you spend any time shopping or dining out in the US, you will see how this principle is being violated by so many as the "me" generation has not been taught anything about loyalty, faithfulness, and integrity. Instead it is all about them and what would profit them the fastest and the greatest. Walk into any fast food restaurant near closing time, and you will see what I mean. I have walked into a fast food restaurant and have had to beg them to take my order. Many times I have been told that they were closed, yet it was still 15 or more minutes before closing time. You can be assured that the owner—who struggled to pay the bills as well as pay the employees who sit around watching the clock—was not there.

As I was standing in line the other day, two employees got into a fight over whose job it was to wait on me. My satisfaction with my visit was not obviously their top priority as they yelled and screamed at each other, "That's not my job!" and, "Well, that's not my area." Those two employees had no clue why they were there. If the owner had been there and heard what was going on, he or she would have labeled them as wicked and lazy. They would have been thrown out on the street. Unfortunately, those two employees are not that rare in today's "me" generation.

In fact, the "hireling" mentality they demonstrated is prevalent in our society. Employees view their time at work as all about them, a temporary situation on the way to where they want to be. They are just there to make a few bucks and then will move on. There is no conscious understanding of the need to make a profit—or even that they have been entrusted with a responsibility. Without the owner present, they believe that they are getting away with doing as little as possible, but what they do not realize is that they are training themselves for failure later on. If only they could get a glimpse of what God would love to do with them. If they could only understood the principle laid out in this parable. If they would take their jobs seriously and apply themselves to be faithful with someone else's property, *then* they themselves would have their own opportunities someday. Just remember this: God knows our hearts. He watches our lives, and He is the one who promotes. *There are no small assignments!*

One day my daughter Amy was sitting at her desk working. She still lived at home at the time, and she had a desk there beside her mother's desk. At the age of 23, Amy held a very high stress job in the ministry. She was the praise and worship leader as well as the creative communications manager. She also wrote a lot of copy and proofread anything that went out from the ministry. As the church grew, we divided those responsibilities out to many others. But at that time, she did it all. She was working long hours and was still single. She saw no prospects in our own church for her husband. She did not really have much time to socialize outside of work and church. But one thing about Amy—she had our heart and she had God's heart. That particular day, as I sat at my desk across the room from Amy's, I saw that she was weeping at her desk. Immediately, the Lord spoke to me and told me to write something down for her. I wrote out an email to her that went something like this:

> Amy, your mother and I thank you for all your hard work. We love you very much, and I want to encourage you today that God knows where you are. As David was faithful in his father's house, it appeared that he was overlooked for promotion and was doomed to watch over sheep the rest of his life. But God saw his heart and his faithfulness. God knew where he was when the prophet was sent to his father's house to anoint a new king over Israel.
>
> The Lord told the prophet that He would show him who the king was to be from the sons present there. But as you know, David's father did not even have him come in from the fields when the prophet came and asked him to have all his sons present. No one even considered that it could be David. But the prophet knew that there must be another son who had not shown up when the Spirit of God did not point out any of the sons that were there. The prophet asked Jesse if he had any more sons. Jesse answered that there was one more, the youngest, who was out with the sheep. The prophet then asked Jesse to call for David. And as you know, Amy, David was indeed the one the Lord had picked.

Amy, you are that David. God knows where you are, and He will not forget your labor and faithfulness. He will bring your husband, and I also will not forget your faithfulness or the love you have shown your mother and I. You can also be sure that God will not forget your heart for His Kingdom either. He will see to it that you get your reward.

I sent the email and saw her open it. She jumped up from her desk and ran over and hugged me, both of us in tears. It was truly a God moment for her and for me.

Later that year, we needed to hire an employee to run the television ministry. Another employee mentioned a friend they knew of in Florida who was looking for a new job and had the experience we needed. We called him and he came to interview with us. We ended up hiring him, a connection only God could have arranged. To make a long story short, Jason and Amy were married a year later. He is everything that Amy desired in a husband and everything I desired in a son-in-law. They both now work in the ministry together, and God has blessed them.

They already have many testimonies. They bought a house this past year for $49,000 that once had appraised for $220,000. The house sits in the country with a huge view of the valleys behind it. Amy's desire was to own a BMW three series sedan, which God brought, and she now owns it debt free. Jason loves Ford trucks, and his truck is also free of debt. Amy and Jason are truly blessed living in the Kingdom and have found that the Kingdom will provide for any need.

Beyond monetary needs, Amy experienced God as her healer, as well. Let me explain. Amy's abdomen had begun to protrude a couple years ago. Multiple doctor's visits had not turned up any answers, and everyone had a different opinion. Strangely, no doctors wanted to do an internal scan. But it got to the point where everyone thought Amy was six months pregnant. The demonic side of this was that Amy had never kissed a man until she stood at the altar with Jason. She ministered to young girls about keeping their innocence. But now everywhere she went, people would ask her when her baby was due. Amy had stopped speaking out as much because she was troubled by the condition. She knew that God healed and had seen God heal many people. She had prayed about this situation several times, as well. But every time she went to the doctor about it, they would say that she was just built that way and there was nothing wrong. This caused confusion for Amy, as she did not know how to believe God. It hindered her from receiving her healing.

I taught a series on healing in our church for about six weeks, and Amy had finally had enough. She did not care what the problem was, or the fact that the doctors were confused as to the cause—she was standing for her healing. She had the elders of the church lay hands on her for her healing, and she started declaring she was healed. About two weeks later she went to bed, in just as much discomfort as ever. But she was shocked when she woke up in the morning to find that she had been healed during the night. She had lost 13 pounds and 9 inches around her waist while she slept. Her spine, which had been too straight with vertebrae sticking out, was now perfectly curved. Her organs, which X-rays had shown as displaced, were back in place. God is always faithful to those that are faithful to Him!

I have a very good friend who owns businesses here in Ohio and is very wealthy, at least in my opinion. He owns two beautiful, lakefront homes here in Ohio and one of the most amazing homes in Florida that I have ever seen. He drives anything he wants, owns all the boats and motorcycles he can use, and is just blessed. Now looking at him, you may be tempted to say, "See that guy? He is failing the money test. He is using all his money to build his estate just like Jesus warned us about." But what you don't see is what I see. This man sows millions of dollars a year into the Gospel. I have seen him write out checks for over $500,000 and pay off a church for a pastor. I could not even begin to name all the ministries that he has supported and continues to support. He absolutely loves the Kingdom, and he has truly passed the money test. You see, God can trust him and rewards him with amazing wealth because he is constantly starting new businesses to propel the Kingdom.

In a recent conversation I had with him, he showed me a new business venture that he was starting. His comments were, "I am starting this business to support the Gospel. I have all I need, but I want to sow more, and I believe that this is another multi-million-dollar business idea." The other day I asked him how his businesses were doing in light of the recent recession that hit America. He told me how his businesses were hitting record-breaking marks every month. He said, "Gary, we are good, but not this good. There is no real explanation as to why we are doing as well as we are doing. What we are seeing is supernatural."

No one starts at this level of wealth and responsibility; they have to be tested first. That test will always start where you are at currently. It will start with your ten dollars, not your future ten million dollars. As I have stated, so many people will tell you that when they have extra money they will be faithful to give it. But in their hearts, any money they are going after is for themselves. They justify the fact that they aren't giving right now by thinking that once they have what they need *then* they will give to God's Kingdom. They are lying to themselves and to God.

What would happen if you viewed money differently?

Jesus told us that we are the managers of our Master's resources. What if we approached our giving to God with the same shrewd business concepts and ideas as we do in trying to gain our own profit? Let me put this in simple terms. What if we viewed the entire purpose of our wealth, the entire reason that we desire money, as a means to help people, making our money fully available for God's purposes? Most of us do it in reverse. We go after the money we need and look at giving to God as something we will do along the way as we can. Giving to God is secondary for most people; it is usually not the principle reason that people want to prosper. I believe if we stop and ask ourselves the question, *"Why do I want to prosper?"* and then truly examine our hearts for an honest answer, we will find that God's purposes may be secondary to our own.

Certainly we *should* believe God for the money to pay for everything we need to take great care of our families. But I believe that if our hearts are for the Kingdom, our giving will show that. I do not believe it is a question of, "Should I use this money for my family or give it to God's purposes?" It's not like it's one or the other. It is a heart issue, and if we purpose in our hearts to be givers, God will bless us so that *we can do both.* I always tell my church that I could gauge where their treasure lies in just a few minutes if they would show me their checkbook. That's because we will always invest where our treasure is. Please know that I am not trying to bring condemnation. I am just trying to illustrate one of the most fantastic money mysteries of life.

So here is the mystery, or we could call it the million-dollar question: **Can you be trusted with money?** Are you just as shrewd toward God's assignments in your life as you are for your own? Again, I want to make this point very clear. Jesus is not telling you to live in financial bondage, with every cent you make going to God's work in the earth realm. He says if you are trustworthy with money, and have a heart to further the Kingdom of God, then God will trust you with more. And if you are faithful with another person's property, you can be trusted with your own.

When I said *yes* to God to start and pastor a church, I knew that I would not have the time to work in my businesses as I once did. I said, "OK, Lord, you take care of my business, and I will take care of Yours." And He has done that consistently over the last 16 years as I have pastored His people. The last three years, in spite of the financial recession, we have had the very best years in business with the greatest income of my entire life. My businesses broke cash flow records, even though most businesses were declining. My church's giving has increased every year since it was founded.

So learn the mystery in the story of the dishonest manager. Are you shrewd for God's profit just as you are your own? Do you have the Kingdom's best interest at heart? Readjust your mindset about money. If you will stop thinking of it as either "yours" or "God's," but instead begin to view all of it as available to God, then you are going to be a very blessed person. If you take care of God's stuff, He will take care of yours!

‖‖

Chapter Eleven

THE MYSTERY OF THE MEASURE

Give and it shall be given unto you. A good measure, pressed down, shaken together and running over.... For with the measure you use, it will be measured to you (Luke 6:38).

IT is amazing how many people have never been taught the principle of the measure. They will sow $10 and expect a $1,000,000 return. That kind of hope will surely be disappointed because, as we have seen in the parable of the talents, God does not give us more than we can manage at a time. If a person has only been faithful in managing $25,000 a year, that person will have to grow and change to be able to handle $10,000,000. *But it is possible* to believe God and grow to that point? The mystery of the measure is really not that complicated if you think of a farmer who sows his seed. His measure is the number of acres that he is planting for that season. Even if his field produced a fantastic crop, his return will still be limited by the measure of his acreage. Likewise, when we sow and believe God, we must understand the principle of the measure. In the same way that a farmer is limited in his harvest, we are limited in our harvest.

To get a picture of this principle, let's go back to our story of Peter and John catching their two boatloads of fish, found in Luke 5. As you remember our discussion in the previous chapters, it was Peter's faith that brought the catch. James and John just came out and helped Peter haul the fish in. We discussed how that was possible through the law of partnership. But let me ask you a question in reference to that story. What if Peter, James, and John would have had 3,000 boats there that day on the lake? How many of them would have been filled with fish? If you said 3,000, then you would be right. But their harvest was limited, not by the law of partnership that was operating, but rather by the number of boats they had available under their legal dominion. The two boats they had were packed so full that the nets about broke and the boats almost sank. There was just no more room for more fish.

But if they would have had thousands of boats at the lake that day, they would have had thousands of boats about to sink from being full of fish. So who limited the catch here? Not God, but rather, Peter, James, and John. It was limited by the measure they had available. The picture of their two boats barely staying afloat with so many fish is a good picture of what it means to have a good measure, pressed down, shaken together, and running over. This illustrates what a "hundred-fold return" really is.

In this story we can see that the measure they gave Jesus—the fishing business—was the measure that was filled. This is a powerful principle that we can see in yet another story recorded in Second Kings 4.

> *The wife of a man from the company of the prophets cried out to Elisha, "Your servant my husband is dead, and you know that he revered the Lord. But now his creditor is coming to take my two boys as his slaves."*

Elisha replied to her, "How can I help you? Tell me, what do you have in your house?"

"Your servant has nothing there at all," she said, "except a little oil."

Elisha said, "Go around and ask all your neighbors for empty jars. Don't ask for just a few. Then go inside and shut the door behind you and your sons. Pour oil into all the jars, and as each is filled, put it to one side."

She left him and afterward shut the door behind her and her sons. They brought the jars to her and she kept pouring. When all the jars were full, she said to her son, "Bring me another one." But he replied, "There is not a jar left." Then the oil stopped flowing.

She went and told the man of God, and he said, "Go, sell the oil and pay your debts. You and your sons can live on what is left" (2 Kings 4:1-7).

I love how this Scripture brings out the principle of the measure. The story makes a point to say that when all the jars were full, she asked for another one, and her son said there were no more. *Then* the oil stopped. Notice the oil stopped after she ran out of jars. What would have happened if she had gathered one million jars? She would have filled one million jars and become the wealthiest woman in history. But as you can see in this story, she was the one who set the measure. God filled the measure that she gave Him to fill. Her measure, the number of pots she gathered, was defined by her. The prophet had already told her to gather many pots, so we can assume that the number of pots she gathered was a large number to her. But if she really had gotten the revelation of what was about to happen, she would have gone to the neighboring towns and gathered thousands of pots. One thing is known, however—she was not ready for the oil to stop filling pots when it did, as was evidenced by her asking for another pot. Then the oil stopped. She set her measure.

Let me tell you why this principle is so important by telling you a story of an associate who worked with me. He was building a home and was trying to build as much of it with cash as he could. During the building process he had planned to pay cash for the kitchen cabinets, but when that time came he was $22,000 short. I remember when he called and we talked about that $22,000. A few weeks later, his wife called and told me what happened. He had attended a ministry conference, and at the end they took up an offering. So my friend went down front, gave some money, and came back to his seat. His wife, however, noticed that when he came back to his seat, he seemed agitated. He sat there for a moment and then got up, went back down, and gave more money. This time when he came back to his seat, she said he seemed even more agitated and bothered. After a moment, he sighed, got up again, went back down to the front and gave more money. This time he gave all he had. When he returned to his seat this time, he was at peace. A few days later, his builder gave him a totally unexpected discount on the cabinets, and he was able to pay for them in cash.

So why am I telling you this? Because without knowing it, my friend was setting the measure. He had asked the Lord for that $22,000, and in that meeting the Holy Spirit was moving on him to give, to set the measure so that God could meet his $22,000 need. How many times have you asked God for the money to pay off your car or your house, and then the next time you are given an opportunity to sow into a ministry project, you suddenly have this wild idea to give a huge amount? The amount scares you and seems so outlandish that you are tempted to laugh out loud. Most people drop the idea right there and go back to their what-fits-my-budget mindset. But what they do not realize is that God was trying to help them set the measure so that they could receive what they had asked Him for.

So let's review. Jesus said that with the same measure that you give it shall be given back to you. Paul also said this in Second Corinthians 9:6, "*Whoever sows sparingly will also reap sparingly, and whoever sows generously will also reap generously.*" Remember our previous discussions about the earth realm and how God is limited here by what people do and allow Him to do? The law of the measure is the law that determines and limits how far God can move in a financial situation. We already saw that satan claims all the money of the kingdoms of the earth as under his domain. Satan would claim foul if God ever breached his legal rights in the financial realm. So it is men and women, and not God, who limit what God can do in the earth realm. People were given the legal authority in the earth realm. That is why both Paul and Jesus said that you receive at the same measure you give. It is a law. However, this law of the measure is not solely based on the dollar amount that you give.

> *Jesus sat down opposite the place where the offerings were put and watched the crowd putting their money into the temple treasury. Many rich people threw in large amounts. But a poor widow came and put in two very small copper coins, worth only a fraction of a penny. Calling His disciples to Him, Jesus said, "I tell you the truth, this poor widow has put more into the treasury than all the others. They all gave out of their wealth; but she, out of her poverty, put in everything—all she had to live on*" (Mark 12:41-44).

Notice that the people who were wealthy were giving large amounts of money, but were giving it out of their excess. How much faith does it take to give out of your excess? Not much. The widow did not give much at all, but her two coins meant more to her, and represented more of her wealth, than what the wealthy folks were putting in. Jesus said that she gave all that she had to live on. How much faith would it take to give all you had to live on? Great faith! Jesus said because of this she gave more than anyone else.

This story shows us that the measure is not set simply by the amount of money that a person gives, but also by the faith released in the giving. This is why God moves on us at times to give what we esteem as an uncomfortable amount. He is helping us set the measure. In my conferences, I try to explain this principle in detail and encourage people to give at a level that requires faith, especially when they want to go to a new level of income. Many times people will ask me how much they should give. I can't answer that for them, but the Holy Spirit will. The key is to give what He shows you to give. Remember, God can't demand that you give your money away, because it is your money. He is not a hard taskmaster. But if you will trust Him, and if you understand the law of the measure, He will lead you in your giving and help you set the measure for the things you believe for.

It will take faith! I have wept as I have given precious seed because the seed was so precious to me. But if you want the kind of testimony that Sharon wrote me about, you will need to understand the law of the measure and how to stand in faith. But as you can see, the victory is so worth it! Here's what Sharon said:

> Pastor Gary, I am writing this on behalf of my husband and I. I just want to start by saying that I thank God for you because you and your wife have been a total inspiration to my husband and I. We heard about you on the Sid Roth show about three or four years ago. We were going through a very difficult time. My husband was fired from his job of 18 years, and we had just built a home for $280,000 dollars. You know that we were up to our neck in debt and stress. We heard about you and ordered your tapes, and that carried us through.

We learned how debt could be so crippling and affect your health and life so poorly. We didn't see a way out, but we lived in that house for two years without paying a mortgage payment. Thank you Jesus, we didn't get thrown out on the street. It's a long story, but I'll make it brief. My husband ended up getting his old job back after four years, because he stayed in faith and believed the promises of God. You and your wife helped us through by listening to your tapes. We ended up purchasing a house for cash after my husband received his job back plus *all his back pay from those four years!*

Sharon and her husband attended my Provision Conference after I received her email, and I had a chance to talk to them at length about what God had done. It was an amazing story! They built their new home, and then they lost it when he lost his job. But they kept confessing the Word, believing that God would vindicate them, as they believed Gary had been wrongfully fired. But they did not hire an attorney or file a lawsuit. Instead they sowed toward God's kingdom and trusted God in that situation. And although it took four years, her husband got the same job back with all of his back pay for the four years that he had not worked. With that huge bonus, they were able to go and pay cash for a bigger home than the one they lost. But the greatest difference in the two houses was that the first one had $280,000 of debt against it, and the second one was paid in full!

In conclusion to this principle, know that the enemy will accuse you of being a fool when you give and stand on the Word of God, but when the harvest comes in, and you are on the way to the bank, you will be the one laughing!

Chapter Twelve

THE POWER
OF FAITH

THE anointing was so strong that I could hardly stand. Everyone in the room was dancing and shouting as they brought their money up front to give into the offering. The ushers holding the bags that the people were putting their money in were weeping and having trouble standing up. I had never seen something like this before, at least not during an offering. I was in Tirana, Albania, in 2005, speaking at a conference that my friend was hosting. He had been in Albania since the country opened to the Gospel 12 years earlier. For the last year, I had felt an urge in my spirit to conduct what I was going to call a Financial Revolution Conference. This was to be a series of five meetings in which I felt I would have the time to lay out some of the Kingdom financial principles that had changed my life. Up until that time, I had never put these principles together in a systematic format. In my spirit, I kept seeing myself conducting a five-session conference on finances. As I was praying about it, I ran into my missionary friend whom I had not seen for a while. He told me about the upcoming conference in Albania and invited me to speak at it.

When I got off the plane in Tirana, he greeted me with an amazing statement: "Gary," he said, "one of my speakers canceled at the last minute, and you are going to do five sessions." My heart jumped. *This is it!* I knew that this was a God appointment, and I would now get to see how the conference I saw in my spirit would play out. I had my notes with me, but had not put them together in a five-session format. So each day I would teach, then go back and pray in the Spirit and write out my notes for the next session.

Before I go any further, I need to tell you that Albania was an extremely poor country at the time I went. The average wage was about $500 a month, and bribery was a way of life for the people. As I thought about teaching the people about finances, I was not sure how they would receive it, but in each session I could see faith growing on their faces. They were hearing the good news of the Kingdom. The evening before the last session I was to teach, the Lord spoke to me that I was to take up an offering for the local churches. I was unsure of this because, first, it was not my conference, and second, I was not sure how the people would respond. We had to pay many of the transportation and housing expenses for the local pastors just to get them to the meeting. I talked to my host friend about it, and he told me to go ahead and take up the offering.

Now, as I watched the people dance and shout with joy as they gave their offering, I was overwhelmed by the anointing and also by the sincere faith of those who were giving such precious seed.

After the service, my friend was obviously moved by what he had seen; he was also surprised by the two stuffed offering bags we were taking back to his apartment from the evening service. He told me that usually when he had collected an offering in the past, only one offering bag would be full. We made our way to his small apartment through the crowded street. When we arrived, we sat down in his living room and opened the offering bags to count the money that had been given to the churches. As Larry dumped the contents of the bags out on the table, something happened that to this day is hard to put into words. All of a sudden a light bluish haze filled the room and the presence of God overpowered us. We sat back under the anointing that filled that place. It was unlike any anointing I had ever felt before, even while I was preaching or praying for people. Instead, this anointing made me feel like I was in the very presence of God Himself. There was a holy, sacred feeling to it. As we sat there, it kept getting stronger and stronger in the room. All we could do was just sit there and weep.

Then I saw, in the middle of the pile of money poured out on the small table, a man's wedding ring. I was overtaken by the fact that someone there that night had no money, but wanted to give so badly that he gave the only thing that was precious to him. The Lord spoke to me at that moment and said:

> I am calling you to the nations to teach them these principles I have taught you about the Kingdom and finances. This ring was put in the offering tonight with great faith. But I want you to take it and keep it as a remembrance of this night. Also, know that just as a wedding band speaks of covenant, you are declaring my covenant of provision to My people. And know that anywhere I send you, I will provide the money to pay for it.

I could not sleep the entire night. I was staying at my friend's apartment that night, and the anointing lingered there. Flying all the way across the Atlantic on the way home, I still could not sleep. All I could do was stare out the window and weep for the entire eight-hour flight. I could not sleep for 46 hours after the Lord spoke to me. For months after that night, whenever I thought of it, I would sense that same presence and begin to weep.

I did not tell my friend what the Lord told me about that ring. The money in the offering belonged to the churches of Albania, and I knew that the ring could be sold for additional money. But I also knew what the Lord told me about it, so I was overjoyed when this missionary friend called me and said the Lord spoke to him and told him to give me that ring as a thank you for speaking to the people of Albania. I mounted that ring, and it is now in my office. There have been many times when I have looked at that ring and had to remember the words the Lord spoke to me that night. I have faced what have seemed like huge financial challenges over the years. Without fail, God has been faithful to provide everything I have needed to walk out His direction to me. That night in Albania changed my life, but there was a lot more that God was going to show me in the days ahead.

When I got home from Albania, I felt a sudden urge to take this message of the Kingdom everywhere I could. I had such a strong passion to get this information out, and I was anxious to teach those same five sessions again to see if the same thing happened. I did not have to wait long. I was invited by a pastor in Utah to come out and teach those same five sessions. He had heard from the Albanian missionary that it was life changing, and so he wanted me to come. He was the pastor of a small, Native American church located on a reservation. It was very poor. They needed help financially, and this pastor said that if what happened in Albania was true, he had to bring it to his church.

So I flew out and held meetings from Sunday morning through Wednesday night. It was five sessions in all, just like in Albania. And I had the same response. The people shouted and danced on the last night of the conference, under a very strong anointing as they gave their offering. I did not see the blue haze this time, but I felt that same strong anointing throughout all five sessions. After the last session I was shocked—just like in Albania—at the large offering that the church, which was comprised of only 17 couples, had given. The offering was sent to my ministry headquarters to process the next day. Later that day, I received a call. One of the ministry secretaries was on the phone, and I could tell something was going on. Her voice was shaking, and it sounded like she had been crying. Her first words were, "Pastor, there is something about that money from the conference." "What do you mean, Tracy?" I asked.

She then went on to tell me that she had opened the moneybag to count and deposit, but the minute she did, the anointing fell in her office. She fell to the floor! Another secretary, hearing the commotion, came around the corner and she too began to shake under the anointing.

Tracy asked me, "What happened with that money out there in Utah?" I told her I did not know. A couple weeks later, I was teaching these same principles in a small church in the southern part of Ohio. In this church, we had sent down the first four sessions by DVD, and they had watched them the previous four weeks. I went down on Sunday night to finish out the five sessions. The anointing was again about to knock us over. When I took up the offering that night, I had the same response as once again the people got so excited to give. During the offering, the church set one basket up front for the people to put their giving in. This time the blue haze was there again. There was an orb about five feet in diameter around the offering basket as the people gave. The anointing was so strong that I had to be helped to the car afterward, as I was unable to walk on my own.

As these things happened, I did not really know what was going on, and I haven't heard of it happening anywhere else. I continued to do conferences, and the anointing continued to be very strong. And yes, that blue haze did show up again in a few conferences. But the part that puzzled me the most was the fact that the anointing was on the money itself. After each conference, my staff had a hard time counting the offering. If you would pick up a piece of money that was given in the offering, you would immediately feel the anointing and begin to shake.

As a spiritual scientist, I was puzzled by all this and asked the Lord about it. He spoke to me and told me that most people give out of duty or legalism. He said as I am teaching His Kingdom and revealing the hidden financial principles of the Kingdom, faith rises in people's hearts, and they are giving in true faith. The Kingdom connection is there, and thus, the flow of the anointing.

As I thought about what the Lord said, I realized that most of the time Christians do give out of duty, habit, or religious tradition and not really out of faith. Most of the financial teaching the Body of Christ hears on giving is not faith-based and portrays God as some kind of magic genie. Without proper teaching, people know nothing other than to beg God to do something that He has already given them legal right to. As I travel the country and the world teaching people about the Kingdom, I do not simply teach them that the Kingdom is their answer. Rather, I teach people that the Kingdom is their answer, and that the laws and principles govern its operation in the earth realm.

So here is yet another money mystery that you need to understand:

Give only when you are in faith.

You must remember that the power of the anointing flows through faith and not formula. For instance, when people first begin to hear the teaching about the Kingdom, they immediately focus on the formula—what I did and how I did it. The reason they do this is simple to understand, and it is a common mistake because the formula is easy to see. People ask me how much they should give and what should they say when they sow. I can answer those questions for them based on what it looks like from my perspective, but following the formula is not necessarily going to produce the results they are looking for. A formula is not the same thing as faith.

One way to determine if you are in faith is to ask yourself if you can defend your position in a spiritual court of law. What Scriptures and truths are you basing your confession and actions upon, and more importantly, do you believe them? Most of the time when it seems faith has failed, you find the person was never in faith to begin with. That is why I believe the Lord led me to teach a five-session series on these principles. It takes some time to lay these things out and for people's hearts to respond in faith. If you would like a copy of the conference that I taught in Albania and have been teaching around the world, it is called *The Now Revolution 2.0*, available at garykeesee.com.

When I experienced that blue haze, and that anointing during the offerings, and saw the extreme results in people's lives when they gave in faith, I realized sadly that most of the Body of Christ is not normally in faith. The average church offerings in America are quite a contrast to what I have seen in conferences. I realized the Body was weak when it came to an understanding of how finances flow, why they flow, and what they are for. I have made it one of my top priorities to help people understand the benefits of the Kingdom they now stand in. I have found God faithful, and His laws never change. God has never failed me financially, *never!*

Even when I was tempted with discouragement, God trained me to trust that He is faithful. God has met my financial needs so many times at the last minute. I have to sometimes remind myself of the mysteries I have been sharing with you. God always comes through, and the last-minute strategy He many times uses is for our good, not our harm. The fear and anxiousness we feel as the clock ticks down the minutes to our deadline is really a result of our own unbelief. I have found that if I were ever going to reach my destiny and run my race, I would have to get comfortable facing fear and circumstances that seem impossible. I must know that God is faithful.

This lesson was made very clear in the early days as Drenda and I were building our house. We were so excited to have our own home after being so financially broke for so long. Our desire was to build the house with cash as we went. Because of that, I was doing much of the work myself. We did our own electric work, flooring, painting, outside tile, landscaping, drainage work, and more. Through the building process, it seemed money was being sucked up right and left, as anyone who has built a house can attest. Bills for this and that just kept coming. I was working late into the night on the house, long hours at the business to produce the money that we needed in the day, and I was getting worn out.

One day I reached a point of despair. I was so tired. I cried out to the Lord in self-pity, and He answered me. "Gary," He said, "how did you think this house was going to show up? I am working with you, and the money and the house are coming together. Know that there will be pressure in every venture that you reach for. If you did not want to tackle the pressure, you could have opted not to build a house." That word was sobering and a gentle attitude correction from the Lord, but it has held true through the years. If you are going to win battles, there will be pressure—don't let that surprise you.

When I now come home to my wonderful house and land, which are paid for, I forget all about the pressure it took to build it. The battle is worth it! I end this book with this one thought, which is not really a money mystery, but a plea from my heart to yours, from someone who has been in the place where it seemed like there was no way out.

Please do not accept mediocrity and complacency for your life. God has equipped you not to be a survivor, but a champion! You are the hero that someone is looking for, the example that God desires to share with the world. With the Holy Spirit's help, you are created to do exploits in the name of Jesus, exploits that will draw the unbeliever to the Gospel.

It is amazing what treasures await you!

Yours for the Kingdom,

Gary Keesee

ABOUT
GARY KEESEE

A few years after their wedding, Gary and Drenda found themselves with a mountain of debt and nowhere to turn. Desperate for real answers to life's toughest questions concerning faith, family, and finances, the Keesees began to get serious about the Bible. It was there they found hope, and through applying sound financial principles, their lives truly changed from the inside out. They paid off all of their debt, made a stronger commitment to their marriage, and rebuilt their financial business, catering it toward helping families live financially free.

Gary and Drenda's strong desire to minister in the marketplace fueled the creation of their many businesses, which are centered around helping people with their finances. Forward Financial Group alone has helped hundreds of thousands of clients, and Gary continues to encourage Christians to go out into the business world and make a difference.

Faith Life Now, founded by Gary and Drenda, offers worldwide conferences, weekly television programming, books and other resources, practical financial support, and personalized help for people who need answers. The Keesees are passionate about getting down to the basics of how to live a different kind of life, and they love to share their stories.

Gary holds a B.A. from Oral Roberts University. Also the pastors of Faith Life Church, the Keesees make their home in Columbus, Ohio, with their five children Amy, Timothy, Thomas, PollyAnne, and Kirsten.

DESTINY IMAGE PUBLISHERS, INC.

"Promoting Inspired Lives."

VISIT OUR NEW SITE HOME AT
WWW.DESTINYIMAGE.COM

FREE SUBSCRIPTION TO DI NEWSLETTER

Receive free unpublished articles by top DI authors, exclusive

discounts, and free downloads from our best and newest books.

Visit www.destinyimage.com to subscribe.

Write to: Destiny Image
                P.O. Box 310
                Shippensburg, PA 17257-0310

Call: 1-800-722-6774

Email: orders@destinyimage.com

For a complete list of our titles or to place an order
online, visit www.destinyimage.com.

FIND US ON FACEBOOK OR FOLLOW US ON TWITTER.

www.facebook.com/destinyimage
www.twitter.com/destinyimage